MY FAVORITE HORROR MOVIE

D1598387

MY FAVORITE HORROR MOVIE

EDITED & CURATED BY
CHRISTIAN ACKERMAN

Published by
Black Vortex Cinema
1800 N. La Brea
Los Angeles, CA 90046

© 2018 CHRISTIAN ACKERMAN

INTERIOR LAYOUT/COVER PHOTO: CHRISTIAN ACKERMAN

COVER DESIGN: JOSH MCKEVITT
JOSHMCKEVITT.COM

JOIN US!

WEB:
BLACKVORTEXCINEMA.COM

FACEBOOK/INSTAGRAM:
@MYFAVORITEHORRORMOVIE

TWITTER:
@MYFAVEHORROR

ISBN: 978-1-7322702-0-6

"I want to give them pleasure. Same pleasure they have when they wake up from a nightmare."

-Alfred Hitchcock

BODY PARTS

SACRIFICIAL APPRECIATIONS

Welcome to this ghoulish collection of horrific memories and cinematic obsessions! I'm a filmmaker, yet while putting this book together, I experienced one of the most fulfilling creative experiences I've ever been a part of. This collection is exactly what I hoped it would be, and it's all due to the infectious passion that my colleagues divulged with demented glee. Thank you to each and every one of them. Thank you to Josh McKevitt, who lent his design eyeball to create the skin of this beast that you so happily peeled back to discover the bloody insides of. Thank you to Ranjinder, my wonderful lady, who was forced to talk to the back of my skull for endless hours as I obsessed over every detail in this tome. Lastly, thank you for joining this ghastly journey into the minds of these talented creators to find out why they became so messed up! I encourage all of you to seek them out online and explore their work. Find them at a horror event near you! We all love to discuss horror! Make sure to watch all of the films worshipped here as well. There are some that I haven't seen and I'm inspired to finally do so! Join the conversation with us online! We'd love to hear about your experiences with YOUR favorite horror film and why it made you who you are!

Christian Ackerman
May 1, 2018
Los Angeles, CA

WE THE FREAKS

A HORROR MANIFESTO
BY
CHRISTIAN ACKERMAN

There are two types of people in this world: those who devour horror films with passionate enthusiasm, and those who are unquestionably, unequivocally, 100% bonafide, grade A authentic, card-carrying wussies.

Now, let's call those wussy humans "The Normals". The Normals sit within the supposedly "safe" walls of their homeowners association, upset that their newly-bought canary yellow furniture doesn't match their fuchsia walls. The Normals don't allow their seven-year-old to watch anything remotely scary in fear that nightmares will haunt them for the rest of their lives. The Normals don't realize that The Silence of the Lambs is actually a horror film. The Normals allow ancient books to dictate what type of art they should and shouldn't experience (even though some of those books contain stories worse than any horror film). The Normals (for some insane reason) don't acknowledge that Gremlins is the world's greatest Christmas movie!

We the Freaks are those who understand that by watching horror, we live the excitement they wouldn't normally experience. We are the thrill seekers. Not the types concerned with jumping out of airplanes or climbing large icy mountains during a blizzard. That shit is for crazy people! We are the ones who sneak into the cemetery late at night and duck behind a tombstone to escape the all-seeing spotlight of a police cruiser. We are the ones who hope that the creepy moonlight stroll through the woods turns into losing our virginity to the hottie from geometry class. We are the ones to know that by watching horror, we get a greater understanding of what it means to be alive and what it's like to die. We understand that our flesh is extremely tender and easily ripped apart. We know that our heads can come clean off with the whoosh of a sharp axe! We are those who understand the boundaries of our flesh and the ease that it can all be taken away.

We take this knowledge with us everywhere in our daily lives. We have that third eye in the back of our heads when we're walking in a creepy neighborhood late at night. We notice the weirdos in the train station and understand what they're capable of. We know to protect ourselves by watching horror films. Although we understand that no evil is worse than the evil committed by our fellow man, those realities are no match to the ferocity and destruction caused by our horror villains. Through their actions, we can witness what humans have been doing to each other for eons, without having to see it in person. When understanding that experience through art, we can work to correct the evils of our fathers by the way we treat each other. You may have already realized that severely war-torn countries rarely produce horror films. They experience enough horror in their daily lives. Because most of us don't have wars on our soil, we need these thrills. This proves that our insatiable need for scary tales is inherent in every fiber of our being; a primal urge in our cranial synapses to have the shit scared out of us!

Even if we do or do not believe in the unknown supernatural beings, we understand that they could be possible. We know that war is terrible, that it shouldn't be worshipped, and a horror that shouldn't be without cause. Actually, we'd rather see the politicians who force others into war fight it out amongst themselves, preferably in a bloody, Running Man-style game show that we can watch in the comfort of our own homes!

Horror films aren't real, but we can take great joy in seeing the on-screen deaths of other humans, because some deserve what they get. Some may think it desensitizes us, but not us.

We still carry empathy for others. This idea is not lost on us. We love to connect with the presently powerless, the unwilling underdog, and the hapless hero because these characters inspire us to transcend those trappings in our own lives.

While we're here, let me be crystal-fucking-clear about this: horror IS art! Don't let them tell you that your drawings of zombies ripping at flesh with their teeth is trash. Don't let them tell you that your comic about demonic-suburban-coroners-who-kill-townspeople-for-the-success-of-their-business shouldn't see the light of day. And don't let them tell you that because you made a horror film, you didn't make art worthy of an Academy Award.

I'm willing to bet that if you're holding this book right now, you're NOT one of The Normals. You're one of us. We're the ones who wear black at weddings, to school, and to our boring cousin's summer pool party. We're the ones that wear eyeliner and nail polish and ride skateboards to school, even if no one around us in our gender does. We are the ones whose resting bitch-face doesn't necessarily mean that we're not having fun. (Because daydreaming about mass decapitation IS fun!) We are the weirdos, the ghouls, the ghosts, the goblins, the Freddys, the Jasons, the Michaels, the Pinheads, the Chuckys, the vampires, the zombies, the werewolves, the demons, the outsiders, and the Freaks!

Deep in the night, in cold blood,

Christian Ackerman

SOYLENT GREEN
BY
CERINA VINCENT

Actress/Writer/Producer
Cabin Fever, Disney's Stuck in the Middle
Power Rangers, Not Another Teen Movie
Twitter/Instagram @CerinaVincent
Facebook: @Official.Cerina.Vincent

"What's your favorite horror film?" I get this question often. I'm grateful to be a part of the wonderfully weird and wild horror community; and with that, for the last 20 years, almost quarterly, in either a podcast, magazine interview, or at a dinner party, someone wants to know this answer.

And I never really know what to say. How can I pick just *one*? Honestly, I give a different answer every time, and I hate that I do that. It feels inauthentic.

So when asked to write out my favorite horror film in the form of an essay? Oh my God. Now I really needed to figure it out.

Decision-making is not one of my strengths in life. I'd like to blame it on the fact that I tend to find the beauty in things. I'm a glass half-full kinda girl-so it's hard to choose when you can see the goodness in any direction. Like how can one pick a favorite food, when sometimes you're in the mood for pizza and other times you're craving poached wild salmon with fresh dill and rosemary roasted potatoes? Or deciding between red nail polish or black...but then you remember how pretty a classic French tip looks? Or the love for the beach versus the love for the mountains or a nice glass of Pinot noir or a dirty vodka martini with blue cheese olives?!? You get my point.

So, I have to choose *one* favorite horror film, and write about it? How the hell am I going to do that?

As I sifted through 30-plus years of movie memories I realized a lot about myself, and this genre.

First, I believe there is a horror spectrum. From horror comedies to films that make you want to puke to films that you lose sleep over....over and over again. Somewhere on that spectrum, I suppose must love cheesy B horror movies, creature films, Bigfoot films, haunted house films, and movies about flesh eating viruses. All of which I've starred in. Obviously, it would be obnoxious to choose any of those as my favorite.

So, as I went through the list of horror films in my mind that moved me, my first gut answer was unequivocally *The Shining*. I LOVE Shelly Duvall. I was a giant *Faerie Tale Theatre* fan. I was obsessed with her as Rapunzel. Obsessed. All I wanted was for my hair to grow super long so I could live in a castle and have a handsome man climb up my braid, marry me, and give me babies. So seeing her as the heroine in *The Shining*, I was already rooting for her. I also believe that every actor would give just about anything to work with Kubrick—he's a genius and it's a pretty perfect horror film. There's nothing else like it.

So, as I pondered what to write in this essay about *The Shining*, I decided to re-watch it. And...it resonated differently with me this time around. Although Stephen King is pretty much a God, and everything he writes seems effortlessly cool and creepy, I had an interesting reaction to Jack's character. He was such a *dick* to Shelly! Maybe it brought up bad memories of my own past relationships with grumpy men, or maybe I'm extra sensitive because we have Trump as a president? Whatever the reason, I couldn't help but realize that Jack is a total misogynistic, emotionally abusive, manipulative, depressed, addict, who's stingy with love and affection, and I decided I hate his character so much that I wanted to choose a different "favorite" horror film. Plus, everyone is going to pick *The Shining*.

So, quickly I wracked my brain for another film that I adored. And then I remembered *JAWS*! Yes, *JAWS* must be my favorite. I watched that film dozens of times as a kid. My little brother and I would rewind it to all the iconic scenes where the score swells and people get yanked under water and bit in half and then we'd reenact it in our own swimming pool using foot flippers for fins. I simultaneously loved it and hated it and couldn't get enough of it. But then I thought, where does that land on the horror spectrum? Is it actually "horror"? Should I choose something that has scary stuff like ghosts? And then I remembered my love affair with…

GHOSTBUSTERS! At the sweet age of nine, I was truly terrified when Sigourney Weaver levitated and said, "There is no Dana, only Zuul." And when the eggs started cooking on the kitchen counter?? Forget it…I was hooked. I loved all the Ghostbusters (Bill Murray was my favorite) and all the ghosts (especially the lady in the library). Hands down, it has to be my favorite horror film.

But then I thought, nah. Is that even "horror?" It scared me as a kid, but as an adult, it's just a comedy, right? I should choose something that truly terrifies me.

So, I thought back to my worst horror movie memory ever. Way back in fourth grade, I watched three of those f*cked up *Poltergeist* films at a stupid slumber party that I didn't even want to go to in my sweet *Strawberry Shortcake* sleeping bag and I was never the same. I didn't sleep for WEEKS. No joke.

Weeks. That movie also stimulated a recurring nightmare I had all throughout my youth—which I've now realized only occurred when I was sleep deprived. But that was the effect of those films. I still remember how nauseous I felt sitting in school because I was absolutely exhausted because I was too scared to fall asleep at night! I drove my parents nuts. Anytime an electrical storm hit my desert hometown of Las Vegas and the TV got all snowy, I would freak out. And when I got braces at 12, part of me was 100% sure that it was just a matter of time before they attacked my face. And the fact that that little girl actually *died* in real life? Forget it. It's too much. I hated that franchise.

Well, then that can't really my favorite, right? Those aren't fond horror movie memories. That was awful. On the spectrum of horror, that fell off the edge for me.

So, I wracked my brain to come up with one that encompasses all. One that brings back visceral memories; that's more frightening than it is funny or cheesy, but not so bad that I can't sleep. I wanted to chose a film that has a strong message and still holds true to being a great film. A film that sucked me in so much and terrified me, but was different and interesting. I thought about the world today and how so much of it seems horrific...(*and then it hit me*). My favorite horror film is...

SOYLENT GREEN. Soylent Green is my favorite. If this doesn't land on the horror spectrum, I'm sorry. But this, *to me*, is true horror. I sat in my parent's bed when I was in fifth grade and watched it with my dad. I may have been a little young for such a concept (given my response to *Poltergeist*), but I recall my dad insisting that I watch it with him. I remember almost every single scene. I remember the comforter on my parent's bed. I remember the time of day and what I was wearing. I was disturbed, disgusted, frightened, and honestly heartbroken as I watched this film about a lifeless, dirty planet barely existing. The movie sucked me into it's filthy world and I was mesmerized and horrified all at once. I was truly scared that this would be our future-and I hadn't even gotten to the end yet! And then...*the end*. The end!?! "Soylent Green is made out of *people*?"

There's no scarier line of dialogue in cinema history then that one. It was haunting then, and sadly, it's even worse now. We are currently living in a time with a president who wants to do nothing about climate change. Our oceans are polluted. Species are dying. We are destroying natural landscape to put in strip malls. Cutting down our rainforests, overflowing land-fills, we are changing our eco system and our food is full of GMO's, and guess what? Cancer-causing, processed SOY is in pretty much everything. Yes, *Soylent Green* may be an exagger-ation for entertainment sake, but it's not far off of what could happen to our planet if we continue down a path of loveless, selfish, mindless, unconscious, unsustainable *horrific* behavior.

Phew! I got there...

With love, light, and screams,
XO, Cerina

A NIGHTMARE ON ELM STREET

BY
JEFFREY REDDICK

Writer/Director/Actor/Producer
Final Destination, Dead Awake,
Superstition: The Rule of 3's
Twitter/Instagram: @JeffreyAReddick

We always tell children to follow their dreams. From a very young age, my dream was to work in the movie industry and make scary movies. The irony is, my dream came true because of a nightmare. A nightmare created by a master filmmaker. A nightmare about a frightening man who wore a dirty red and green sweater. A man with knives for fingers. He was terrifying on so many levels. His flesh was horribly burned. He had a wicked cackle that showed the twisted joy he felt when he toyed with and killed his prey. This evil man would mutilate himself just to see the horror in his victim's eyes. His name was Fred Krueger. (Freddy to his friends.) And as embodied with ferocious abandon by Robert Englund, he is one of the most iconic creations to slash his way across the silver screen, in one of the best horror films ever made.

As a pre-teen, the subtext of horror films was lost on me. All my friends and I cared about was the double forbidden fruit of nudity and gore. But at the age of 14, I sat with two of my best buddies, Calvin Saum and Tony Calhoun, and we watched Wes Craven's masterpiece, *A Nightmare on Elm Street*. It isn't hyperbole to say that this film changed my life forever, both personally and professionally. In hindsight, this was the type of unique movie that a filmmaker clearly poured his heart and soul into making.

On a minuscule budget, Wes Craven created astonishing visual effects and reality-bending set pieces that had never been seen before. But more importantly, he brought evil to the suburbs. From the opening frame to the last, there's not a wasted moment in this film. We start with an unseen man, rasping for breath, as he fashions a gleaming, claw-like glove. We see him chase a beautiful young woman through a nightmarish landscape. This young woman, the sharp, tough and funny Tina Gray, was the quintessential leading lady. She had a tight circle of friends, including her rebel boyfriend, Rod, a warm and caring bestie, Nancy, and Nancy's sensitive jock boyfriend Glen. After the intriguing set up and meeting some relatable and likeable characters, we slowly learned that these friends were dreaming about the same terrifying man. It was a great reveal and we were sure Tina would have to battle this fiendish monster to save herself and her friends.

But then Wes Craven did something shocking. He killed Tina in one of the most amazing set pieces ever committed to film. And just like Freddy shredded the woman we thought was our heroine, Wes shredded our expectations about what was going to happen in this film.

Nancy, the quiet and caring best friend, was galvanized by her friend's death and went from the spunky girl-next-door to a brilliant fighter, who had to outsmart and outfight this relentless villain. With Nancy, the horror genre got its first truly proactive heroine, who went after the killer with a mixture of intelligence and fearlessness we weren't used to seeing.

A Nightmare on Elm Street has carved its rightful place on most top 10 lists of the best horror films of all times. Not only for the reasons I've mentioned, but because each element of the film worked perfectly to craft a masterpiece. Look at the stunning cinematography by Jacques Haitkin. Listen to the unique score by Charles Bernstein. During the nightmare scenes, see how all of these elements were blended together, along with the complex sound design that expertly mixed the eerie sounds of children crying, sheep bleating, victim's voices whispering in the wind and that unmistakable sound of metal scraping metal that heralded the arrival of everyone's worst nightmare.

I devoured this movie as a 14-year-old and it cemented my desire to do horror movies for life. I memorized the dialogue. Acted out scenes. And decided to write a prequel and send it to Bob Shaye, who ran New Line Cinema, the studio that produced the film.

I got a standard rejection letter because the treatment was unsolicited. So, I did what any 14-year-old hillbilly with no knowledge of how the film industry worked would do…I wrote Bob a surly response. I explained that I had watched three New Line movies and spent five dollars of my hard-earned money on his stuff, so the least he could do was take five minutes and read my work. Thankfully, he read the treatment and wrote me back. He said I had a fertile imagination, but kindly told me that I needed to work on story structure. For me, this was all the encouragement I needed. I didn't know anything about the business, but I started reading scripts sent to me by Joy Mann, Robert's assistant. I stayed in touch with Joy and Bob for years. When I was a sophomore in college, I went to New York for a summer acting program and got an internship at New Line. I ended up working there for over a decade and they produced *Final Destination.* I had the blessing of working at the company during its creative peak. Sadly, we lost Joy Mann, a wonderfully strong and loving woman. But because I was blessed to count her as a dear friend, she and Bob Shaye taught me what it was like to work at a studio ran by film lovers and not number crunchers. Like my career, New Line Cinema was affectionately known as "The House That Freddy Built."

At the time of its release, *A Nightmare on Elm Street* was described as "fantasy terror." That label, and subgenre of horror, is what I love to write. *Final Destination* is grounded in our real fear of death, but has the fantasy element of Death being a living, intangible force. It was a tough sell to convince a studio to make a movie about Death killing people. I got rejected numerous times. But when I read about how every studio in Hollywood passed on *A Nightmare on Elm Street* (including New Line) before Bob Shaye finally decided to take a chance on this "crazy idea," it kept me going.

So, the movie not only inspired me creatively and spurred my full throttle jump into horror, but the story of Wes' tough journey to bring his dream-child to life, kept me going when I doubted myself. The film also showed me that when creating a horror film, the sky, and your imagination, is the limit. Anything you can imagine on the page can be brought to life with a dedicated director, cast, and crew. And it showed me that sometimes, when you follow the dream that no one else believes in, you can catch lightning in a bottle and create a film that haunts the dreams of viewers for decades.

The devastating loss of Wes Craven was a huge blow to the film community. And although he left behind an impressive body of work, *A Nightmare on Elm Street* is woven into world's DNA. His creation, that Fedora-wearing killer, will never be forgotten and will always be my favorite horror film.

THE TEXAS CHAIN SAW MASSACRE
BY
FELISSA ROSE

Actress/Producer
Sleepaway Camp, Victor Crowley, Death House
Camp Dread, The Perfect House, Satan's Playground
Twitter: @Felissa_Rose Instagram: @FelissaRose123
Facebook: @Felissa.Miller

My all-time, absolute favorite horror movie is the original *The Texas Chain Saw Massacre*. My first time being acquainted with it was when I saw an ad in a local newspaper. I thought, wow, this image with Leatherface holding the chainsaw is so striking and so scary, it actually looks real! The thing that struck me the most was, I wasn't quite sure if it was a documentary or a regular film. My little 13-year-old brain sort of took its own dark turn into what truly felt like the scariest thing I had ever laid my eyes on.

Fast forward to later that fall, I was cast in the horror movie *Sleepaway Camp*. I really wasn't into watching horror, but after making one, I finally felt like I had the stomach to endure one. So of course, the first horror film I decided to see was *The Texas Chain Saw Massacre*! It blew my mind in so many ways! Just the acting itself was superb and unlike anything I had ever seen before! Marilyn Burns quickly became my hero. I thought she was one of the all-time greatest actresses. While her character Sally was forced to endure such a disgusting scenario, her portrayal was so authentic, so vulnerable, and so beautiful to watch, I was mesmerized. Ed Neal as the hitchhiker also blew me away; and (obviously) Gunnar was the most captivating of all!

Many years later, I occasionally worked for *Fangoria*, going to movie sets and conducting interviews. I eventually got to go to the *Chain Saw* thirtieth anniversary reunion at the actual film set in Texas with Marilyn, Gunnar and Ed. As I interviewed the three of them, the fangirl in me couldn't tell whether I was crying or laughing or what my emotions were! They were all so genuinely kind in telling me stories, how they felt about making the movie, and how they all loved it. What struck me the most about meeting them was how, after all those years, they were still such a strongly bonded family. I understood that connection from being a part of *Sleepaway Camp*. Making a film can be very stressful, but when you're around a great group of people in a secluded place, you form a bond with them that lasts forever.

Ed Neal eventually became a good friend of mine after we had some crazy scenes together in a movie called *Satan's Playground*. His character was emotionally and mentally unstable, so he captured and dragged me down to his mother's basement, where he tied me up and put a machete to my throat. It was wonderful working with this icon who I had admired for so many years, and just a dream to work with him in that capacity.

A few short years ago, I did a convention at Connecticut Horror Fest, where I reconnected with Gunnar and became good friends with him. He told me about this dream project he had called *Death House*, and fortunately, I became involved in producing it! But just a few months before we started shooting, he passed away. The team was devastated, but we knew we had to continue making the film in his honor, with the spirit of his dream giving us strength.

Both Gunnar and Marilyn were such kind and sweet souls; so completely different from the characters they portrayed. It was an honor to have known them.

The Texas Chain Saw Massacre will always leave a huge mark on me because I saw that brutal first poster image at such a young age. But actually seeing the movie blew my mind in so many amazing ways. After becoming close with the cast and getting to make Gunnar's *Death House*, *TCM* is now such a part of my entire being that I have nothing but immense love for it. It's definitely my favorite horror movie for so many reasons; from the cast, to the script, to the authentic reality. That's what's so beautiful about the movies of that era. Since they were shot on film, you feel like you're watching this craziness actually unfold right before your eyes. Sort of like life, but (hopefully) without the chain saws!

HALLOWEEN
BY
SEAN JAMES DECKER

Journalist/Screenwriter/Producer
Fangoria, DreadCentral.com,
Yummy Meat: A Halloween Carol
Facebook: @Sean.Decker

In October of 1978, like most eight-year-old American boys of the time, and well before it would become a hip moniker to attach to one's self, I was I suppose what people would consider a "film nerd." I inherited this gene from my father, who had spent his own adolescence religiously attending matinees at the Bayview Theatre in San Francisco, ingesting a steady stream of serials, cartoons and 1950s sci-fi, horror and westerns, which he then imparted to me via network (at the time, we hadn't yet purchased that very expensive new thing called a videocassette recorder) and local television, the latter portal consisting primarily of horror host Bob Wilkins' KTVU show *Creature Features*. (A year later, I'd go on to innocently hold hands with my first girlfriend, the daughter of John Stanley, the latter who had taken over hosting duties of the show: she soon broke up with me for my obsession with her father and his extensive horror collection, but that is another story).

As much as my own father was excited to share with me the films he'd grown up on, from Universal's classic *The Creature from the Black Lagoon* to that wonderful giant ant film *Them!*, he was also as equally concerned at guarding my innocence. When George Romero's *Night of the Living Dead* made its television premiere on Wilkins' show, I wasn't allowed to watch it, although my parents were more than happy to take me to multiple screenings of *Star Wars*, and to support my interest in all things pop culture related via subscriptions to Marvel Comics titles (I remember fondly the brown paper mailing sleeves they'd arrive in), a million Legos bricks, Mego Dolls (I wonder whatever happened to my glow-in-the-dark Human Wolfman), Hardy Boys books, and much, much more.

R-rated horror films though? They were strictly *off the table*, no matter how I pleaded.

That was until my father's dad (who I referred to as "Papa," as we all did), who I spent every other weekend with, often flying the skies above Half Moon Bay in his Cessna when not attending Saturday Mass or the San Francisco Zoo, offered to take me to see a revival screening of 1974's Godzilla Vs. Mechagodzilla, playing in a single screen movie house in the city. Gleefully, I took the street car with him to the theatre for some kaiju G-rated fare, and arriving early, he bought us both popcorn and Cokes and suggested we sit down to watch the end of whatever was playing in anticipation of the Big G's onscreen arrival.

And it was then that my life was forever changed.

In that darkened theatre and through my boyhood fingers, raised in an effort to shield my eyes from the utter terror which was unfolding before them, I watched as a plucky young girl named Laurie crossed a tree-lined street before entering a structure similarly darkened. Up the stairs she went, and fearfully I went with her, into a dimly-lit bedroom where a woman lay splayed out dead on a mattress, a flickering jack-o-lantern next to her and a tombstone above with the inscription "Judith Myers" cut into it. And soon other things would also be *cut into*, by a methodical, shambling shape with a massive butcher knife, who stalked our misfortunate heroine from room to room and house to house, and who while seemingly in the finale was brought down by gunfire by an elderly man in a trench coat with a curious penchant for scaring trick or treaters, would ultimately disappear into the very night, and into my very psyche.

Silent. Unstoppable. Ghostly. For me, without context, and now existing behind every fence in my suburban neighborhood. As for the following screening of director Jun Fukada's *Godzilla* film? I don't recall it. What I do recall are the nightmares scored by that 10/8 piano composition that plagued me in the ensuing weeks, of which I'd wake from, drenched in sweat and screaming, comforted by my concerned parents who were none too happy that my grandfather had taken me to, "That *Halloween* movie" (they themselves made a trip to the theatre shortly thereafter, more than likely in an attempt to understand what emotional trauma their previously unsullied son had endured).

Marvel Comics didn't interest me much after that, although EC Comics did. And while I was certainly excited to see the follow-up to that *Star Wars* movie, I was more thrilled to watch the slasher flicks on Laserdisc which one of my schoolyard chum's father had amassed (a format now primarily residing in landfills alongside that Bakelite phone which Michael used to strangle Lynda Van Der Klok), when we were left to our own devices. Sean Cunningham's gory take on *Halloween*, *Friday the 13th*, was one of them, but in my mind, nothing could compare to the sheer ferocity of Carpenter's film.

I was hooked, and it was merely the beginning. Unbeknownst to my parents, Curtis Richards' novelization was hidden beneath my mattress (I still have that paperback, dog-eared and rag-tag from countless readings), and while I was allowed to see the television cut of *Halloween* when it premiered on NBC in in 1981, I had to sneak into a theatre to see Carpenter's follow-up, *Halloween II*, that same month. Thrilling, yes, but for me even then, it failed to replicate the visceral, German Expressionism-influenced elegance of the original (not that I knew what German Expressionism was at the time, or a Panaglide for that matter).

That first iconic film, written in just ten days and originally entitled in script form the pulpy *The Babysitter Murders*, shot for a mere $320,000, featuring a killer in a modified William Shatner mask purchased for a buck ninety-eight at Bert Wheeler's now defunct magic shop on Hollywood Boulevard, coupled with my parents' encouragement of my early interest in writing, would lead to just that, from my beginnings as an editor two decades later at Universal Studios' Horror Online, to eight years as a writer at the beloved *Fangoria*, to a decade of journalism at Dread Central, with a few produced films and screenplays peppered throughout.

As for *Halloween* and my continued fascination with it, over the course of my career I've had the distinct honor of meeting Carpenter himself, as well as that young, plucky babysitter, and the knife-wielding madman who assailed her. In fact, in my possession at the time of this writing is a vintage Lamson butcher knife, signed by all three. (Curtis' written-in-Sharpie signature and message of "Happy Halloween" is still to me is as surreal as the moment in which she signed it, although no more so than when John did the same in his living room, while allowing me to prattle on to him about his film's resonance, as if he were unaware). And in 2015, and in an interesting turn of events, I nearly portrayed the iconic killer in a proposed San Diego Comic Con teaser for filmmaker Marcus Dunstan's aborted Dimension feature, *Halloween Returns*.

Why me, you ask? Because as Dunstan was gleefully aware, for the past half a decade, each year on Halloween, I've donned a custom-made, screen quality jumpsuit and mask, and to the delight and often sheer terror of those evening's trick or treaters, stalked Orange Grove Avenue in West Hollywood: the very street which Laurie traversed on the flickering screen in that San Francisco cinema so many years ago before my terrified, eight-year-old eyes.

After all, everyone's still entitled *to one good scare*.

PSYCHO
BY
TONY TIMPONE

Writer/Producer/Editor
Fangoria Magazine, Fangoria Radio, Monsterpalooza,
Fantasia Film Festival, Horror Equity Fund
Twitter: @TonyTimpone1

People like this book's editor, Christian Ackerman, always ask me, "What is your favorite horror film?" and the answer has not changed for the last 40 years. No big surprise here, as it's a favorite I share with countless horror and film fans. So in honor of this enduring classic, allow me to salute the greatest horror film ever made with my "Top 50 Reasons Why *Psycho* Is My Favorite Horror Film."

1. The opening titles (disjointed text racing across the screen and being split apart) by the great Saul Bass (*Vertigo, Cape Fear, Seconds*), who also helped design the film's murder scenes.

2. The opening title music by Bernard Herrmann, immediately setting the mood.

3. The taboo-breaking hanky-panky nooner between Marion Crane (Janet Leigh) and Sam Loomis (John Gavin), hooking up in a Phoenix hotel room.

4. Leigh in the white bra and slip. She's a hottie, and we can see where daughter Jamie Lee Curtis got her looks. But besides the sex appeal, Leigh is a damn fine actress (she garnered a Best Supporting Actress Oscar nomination for *Psycho*), making her larcenous character complex and sympathetic.

5. And for the girls, bare-chested hunk Gavin, oozing pure machismo. It's no surprise that the actor tested for the role of James Bond at some point in his career.

6. Perky Pat Hitchcock (Hitch's daughter) as the office secretary/busybody.

7. Actor Vaughn Taylor as humorless bank manager Mr. Lowery, who just wants the missing money back.

8. Frank Albertson as randy Texas oilman Cassidy, he of the loose lips and owner of the fateful $40,000. The actor also appeared in everything from *Man Made Monster* to *It's a Wonderful Life*.

9. Crane/Leigh, now the "bad girl," in sexy black lingerie after she steals the dough.

10. The scene where Marion, in her getaway car at the stoplight, sees her boss crossing the street directly in front of her. Will he confront her? A simple but effective moment of patented Hitchcock suspense.

11. Marion, driving late at night, the voices in her head playing out the discovery of her crime.

12. The creepy highway patrolman (Mort Mills), symbolizing Hitch's childhood fear of authority.

13. Marion's gutsy retorts to the cop, arousing suspicion and, again, creating viewer tension.

14. Character actor John Anderson (quadruple original *Twilight Zone* player) as California Charlie, the least pushy used car salesman you will ever meet. Wish they were all like that.

15. The sharp B&W cinematography of reliable TV DP John L. Russell (*Thriller, Alfred Hitchcock Presents, The Munsters*, etc.). His lens captures every shadow, raindrop and show-

er spray.

16. Marion meeting the shy, boyish and innocent-looking Norman Bates (Anthony Perkins) for the first time.

17. The Bates' creepy, Victorian Gothic mansion on the hill, the ultimate old dark house (designed and built by art director Joseph Hurley and production designer Robert Clatworthy).

18. Those creepy taxidermied birds in Norman's office.

19. Norman's line: "My hobby is stuffing things. You know—taxidermy."

20. Norman's line about Mother: "She just goes a little mad sometimes. We all go a little mad sometimes. Haven't you?"

21. Norman's line: "A boy's best friend is his mother."

22. The flushing toilet. Hard to believe, it was a taboo in Hollywood's olden days to show a commode, let alone seeing it flush on screen.

23. The shower scene, of course. Those 45 seconds combined represent one of cinema's greatest achievements (and the subject of the excellent documentary 78/52). Marion's murder still packs a wallop.

24. The blooper. Even *Psycho* has one! After Marion falls out of the shower stall and the camera closes in on her "lifeless" face, look at Leigh's throat on the bottom left of the frame: You can see the actress swallow!

25. Norman cleans up. It's almost as sick-making as the big kill, as we see the dutiful son mop up the bloody mess that Mother has made.

26. Norman dumping Marion's car in the swamp. We wait with bated breath as the vehicle slowly sinks in the water, then get even more nervous when the auto's descent stalls. Are we rooting for Norman Bates?

27. Vera Miles as Lila Crane. We admire the no-nonsense, feisty, gutsy sister of Marion. Her own journey will presage the final girls and scream queens to come decades later.

28. The kooky old lady (Helen Wallace) in Sam's hardware store who, while buying bug poison utters the macabre line, "Insect or man, death should always be painless."

29. Martin Balsam as Milton Arbogast, the quintessen-

tial private detective. He's a smarmier version of Peter Falk's Columbo. He won't be rewarded for his persistence.

30. Norman's line: "Uh-uh, Mother-m-mother, uh, what is the phrase? She isn't quite herself today."

31. Under moonlight, Norman's face in partial shadow, in the back of the motel by the swamp.

32. Sheriff Al Chambers and his wife. Westerns actor John McIntire and Lurene Tuttle play these stock characters like they just stepped out of an Andy Hardy or Frank Capra movie, but they are ingratiating.

33. The murder of Arbogast. For this viewer, the detective's shocking stabbing on the stairs of the Bates' house is the scarier of *Psycho*'s two slayings because we really don't see it coming.

34. Sam and Lila going all *Hardy Boys/Nancy Drew* at the Bates place. Especially love Sam's needling of Norman and watching the fidgety man crack under the pressure.

35. Lila meets Norma Bates. Again, one of the scariest moments in scream history—Mother's rotted corpse revealed.

36. Those unearthly howls and screams from Norman and Lila, respectively, accompanied by Herrmann's strings. As Norman enters the cellar dressed as Mother, amidst the shrieking Herrmann strings, you can hear the line of dialogue, "I am Norma Bates." Still blood-curdling.

37. The Mother prop. The mummy skin pulled tight across the sneering, eyeless skull, the old lady wig…frightening work by Robert Dawn, who closed out his career on John Carpenter's *Christine*.

38. Future Vincenzo of *The Night Stalker* fame, Simon Oakland, as psychiatrist Dr. Richmond, clinically explaining Norman's psychosis to the other characters and the audience. It's pure exposition, but some of us like having everything spelled out.

39. Mother's final line, "Why, she wouldn't even hurt a fly."

40. The subliminal shot of Mother's desiccated skull over Norman's face in the jail room.

41. The blood-freezing voice of old crone Mother, a combination of three separate performers: Virginia Gregg, Jeanette

Nolan and Paul Jasmin (a male pal of Perkins!).

42. Psycho's solid editing by one of Hitch's greatest collaborators, George Tomasini (*The Birds*, *Vertigo*, *Rear Window*).

43. The screenplay by Joseph Stefano, who improved on Robert Bloch's pulpy novel by changing Norman from a fat, alcoholic middle-aged man into the character we know and love, plus coming up with the memorable dialogue.

44. Herrmann's all-strings music, one of the best film scores ever.

45. Psycho's trailer. Hitch himself hosted the macabre coming attractions preview (written by James Allardice, who also penned his witty *Alfred Hitchcock Presents* wraparounds). No film footage is revealed in the six (!) minute spot, but it did a great job helping to entice $15 million worth of business during Psycho's initial run.

46. Spawned the better-than-expected *Psycho II* 23 years later, directed by Richard Franklin and scripted by *Fright Night*'s Tom Holland.

47. Nicely shot by Bruce Surtees, the flawed but watchable *Psycho III* (1986) put Perkins in the director's seat, and he channeled the Master in a tingly scene with an icebox, a dead body hidden within and a prying sheriff (Hugh Gillin).

48. Mick Garris' direct-to-cable *Psycho: The Beginning* (1990), at the very least, brought original scripter Stefano back into the fold.

49. Anthony Perkins: in his career defining (and destroying?) role, the actor plays the granddaddy of all screen maniacs. Except, unlike all the others, we like him. We really, really like him.

50. Alfred Hitchcock: the greatest director who ever lived, making the greatest horror film of all time.

GOJIRA
BY
MIGUEL DAVID RODRIGUEZ

Film Festival Director/Podcaster/Host
Horrible Imaginings Film Festival & Podcast,
Mass Hypnosis Podcast, Film Geeks San Diego
HIFilmFest.com
Facebook: @HorribleImaginings Twitter: @HIFilmFest
Instagram: @Horrible_Imaginings

"Who could imagine such a thing? Human skin, floating, surviving, still in the bloom of agony. And stones. Burned stones,
shattered stones. Anonymous locks of hair, that Hiroshima's
women, when they awoke, discovered had fallen out."
-Alain Resnais's *Hiroshima Mon Amour*

"The theme of the film, from the beginning, was the terror of
the bomb. Mankind had created the bomb, and now nature
was going to take revenge on mankind."
-*Gojira* producer Tomoyuki Tanaka

In 1985, when I was about seven years old, my father took me to the theater to see what was then called, appropriately, *Godzilla 1985*. This is one of my clearest early cinema-going memories. As with many children that age, I loved dinosaurs. I had books about them, and would proudly boast my knowledge about their names and attributes to any adults who would listen. This was probably the reason my dad figured I would enjoy going to see *Godzilla 1985*, and he even got me a souvenir magazine for the film beforehand.

"What is Godzilla?" I asked my father.
"He's a dinosaur," he answered.
"He is?"
"He's a Tyrannosaurus Rex."

I looked at the cover of my souvenir magazine. Godzilla, with large stalactite teeth jutting beneath a curled snarl, had clawed hands raised almost in a boxer stance over a skyline of explosions, jet planes, and the spaceship-like Super X. I knew T-Rex, and this was not a T-Rex. The head certainly wasn't right, and look at Godzilla's hands! They were huge! As much as I revered the king of the dinosaurs, I knew he wouldn't stand an icicle's chance in Hell against the King of the Monsters. My dad's well-meaning answer was unsatisfactory, and my obsession with Godzilla (and trying to figure out exactly what he was) had begun.

I had little suspicion just how shocking the real answer could be.

I spent my childhood watching VHS copies—mostly what my mom could borrow free from the library—of any Japanese giant monster, or "daikaiju," movies I could find. At that time, this was a limited number and was generally relegated to the campier monster battle films of the later Showa Era: *Godzilla Vs. Megalon*, *Godzilla Vs. The Sea Monster*, *Godzilla Vs. The Smog Monster*, *Godzilla Vs. MechaGodzilla*, and the like. I developed a taste for these and the playground conversations they would inspire, but none of them really captured the feeling of seeing *Godzilla 1985* in the cinema or holding that magazine in my hand.

In all those movies, Godzilla's role and definition was constantly shifting. Was he an animal? A monster? A superhero? It was always a different and (to my younger mind) somewhat unsatisfactory answer until years later when I was able to get my hands on a very expensive bootleg copy of the original Japanese *Godzilla* film from 1954. This also happened to be right around the time I was learning about The Manhattan Project and the bombs Fat Man and Little Boy that reduced two Japanese cities to rubble. The answer to what Godzilla really was became terrifyingly clear, and forever shaped how I watched films.

It is impossible to overstate the revelation that seeing the Japanese original cut of *Godzilla*, or *Gojira*, had been for me. I had seen the American-released *Godzilla, King of the Monsters*, but the changes to the film went far beyond the addition of scenes featuring Raymond Burr. To emphasize this, even with those additional scenes, *Godzilla, King of the Monsters* is still a full 14 minutes shorter than *Gojira*. Where *Godzilla, King of the Monsters* is a fun *Beast from 20,000 Fathoms*-style monster movie, *Gojira* is a film about the very real terror and anxieties plaguing a nation just barely in the recovery process from the bombings of Hiroshima and Nagasaki not even a decade earlier. Suddenly, I was thinking less about my own fun with a rampaging giant monster (and some of the catharsis that could provide), but I began thinking more about the kinds of fears other people were trying to express through that monster.

The creative team behind *Gojira* had first-hand experience with the aftermath of those bombs, including director Ishiro Honda who had barely survived the Tokyo firebombing before finding himself in what was left of Hiroshima—an experience that would forever affect him. "Ever since," he once said, "I felt that this atomic fear would hang around our necks forever."

This experience is felt throughout his direction of the film, which is shot in a straightforward, almost documentary style to depict scenes that would have been agonizingly familiar to the Japanese audiences of the time: sirens blasting, evacuations, a skyline of smoldering husks where a city once stood, overburdened hospitals tasked with caring for survivors who set Geiger counters buzzing. What makes the horror more potent, though, is that it reflected more than just the bombs that had already dropped.

It was no mistake to open the film with a small fishing boat suddenly bathed in a blinding radioactive light. It was a scene ripped right from the headlines. On March 1 of the very same year that *Gojira* was released, the crew of a tuna fishing boat called *Daigo Fukuryū Maru*, or *Lucky Dragon #5*, described a similar blinding flash before being snowed on by radioactive ash. All members got radiation sickness. When it was revealed that this incident was the result of American Castle Bravo hydrogen bomb testing on the Bikini Atoll in the Marshall Islands, any fading memories of Hiroshima and Nagasaki were reawakened with renewed vigor. It had been nine years since the bombings, and only two years since the end of US occupation of Japan, but the continued threat of nuclear weapons seemed stronger and more unrelenting than ever. When *Lucky Dragon 5* radioman Aikichi Kuboyama died as a result of this incident in September, hundreds of thousands of people attended his funeral. *Gojira* was released to the public just two months later, the painfully evocative opening scene including a lingering shot of the boat's radioman furiously tapping a Morse code message before the flaming boat sinks below the bay. This scene is, for me, a truer way to connect to the emotions of the people who were affected by this news in Japan than just reading it as a statistic or a history lesson. This was a way to feel. To understand.

Gojira, then, is not just about remembering the terror of the bombs, but about living with the anxieties of what is yet to come. There are several telling lines in the Japanese version that were either cut whole cloth from the American version or simply left untranslated, all of which clearly refer to the horrors of the new nuclear reality after 1945. When a mother clutches her small children as a building collapses around them, she begs them not to be afraid as they will "see their father soon." When scientists and press investigate the destruction of Odo Island, the actual word "fallout" is used, and seems conspicuously excised from the English dialogue of the US version. The scenes of destruction in their aftermath are what differentiate the 1954 film *Gojira* from other monster movies and even later *Godzilla* films. While those typically revel in the carnage as cinematic spectacle, this one laments them. The score by Akira Ifukube exudes tragedy, rather than thrill. The effects work by master Eiji Tsuburaya, honed from years of doing propagandistic war films, takes great pains to ground the fantastic and absurd in dark and familiar locales. The fallout, both literal and figurative, is depicted at a human level here.

As I have gotten older, I have noticed even more subtext and meaning behind my favorite horror film. For example, it goes beyond just the immediate threat of surviving nuclear war. There is also something terrifying about how easily these horrors can be normalized, how even a threat this existential can become just another nuisance of living. In another significant scene cut from the U.S. version, three commuters discuss the newspaper headline they just read about Godzilla in much the same way anyone discusses bad news on the way to work. "Contaminated tuna and radioactive fallout, and now this Godzilla to top it all off," one person complains. "What if he appears out of Tokyo Bay?" And, much like many of us will do, the other commuter tries some dark humor. "He'll probably go after you first!" Then, things get more explicit. "I barely escaped the bombs at Nagasaki, and now this?" "Evacuate again? I've had enough!" It has clearly gone beyond just the fear of a singular historic bomb and evolved into a here-we-go-again kind of cynical resolve for the everyday Japanese person. And then there is poor Shinkichi.

Shinkichi is a young character whose story almost seems incidental to some of the other character melodrama (a love triangle, a scientist at odds with the military approach to dealing with Godzilla, political strife). He was a resident of Odo Island, which is where we first see Godzilla turn up after destroying the village there, and Shinkichi's family with it. This scene is devastating, as the young man lies helplessly screaming in the typhoon of Godzilla's wake as his family is crushed in their house under the step of the monster. The extremity of his anguish is keenly portrayed by actor Toyoaki Suzuki, in an intentional shot by director Honda. Later, after the orphaned Shinkichi is forced to witness, yet again, the destruction of Godzilla, Honda chooses to linger on his reactions, this time reduced to the same kind of cynical resolve tinged with rage, merely shutting his eyes and whispering, "Damn. Damn." I have often felt like I can relate to Shinkichi in that moment, when the troubles of the world seem so impossible that bowing my head in despair seems like a reasonable response. But Shinkichi is not the only character, and we get some alternate reactions to bite into.

A large part of the message I take from *Gojira* is to take care to guard ourselves against this kind of numbness. The scientist Serizawa, forced to live with an eyepatch due to a hinted-at injury from "the war," toils away like a recluse in his lab. He is the film's Oppenheimer, who possesses a weapon of mass destruction, but refuses to tell anyone about it lest another cataclysm happen. When the threat of Godzilla forces his hand to implement the weapon, he sacrifices himself to maintain his secret. His friend and colleague, Dr. Yamane (played by the legendary Takashi Shimura, or, as NY Film Forum's Bruce Goldstein called him at the TCM Film Festival presentation of *Godzilla*: "the leader of the frickin Seven Samurai!"), wears a face of sad understanding at Serizawa's sacrifice. This scene is another one in which 1954's *Gojira* is set apart from other giant monster films. The survival of humankind is met not with triumph and trumpet blasts, but with tragedy and reflection. Dr. Yamane's final words, "if we continue conducting nuclear tests, it's possible that another Godzilla might appear somewhere in the world again," are in stark contrast to the more optimistic final line uttered by Raymond Burr in the U.S. version: "the whole world could wake up and live again!"

Now, as an adult, I can understand that Godzilla has become a concept more than anything else—an idea that can morph to fit the changes, anxieties, concerns, or just plain entertainment wants of the times. The thematic needs he served in 1954 are different than from those in 2016 when *Shin Gojira* was released, but that just makes the perspective of that first film all the more potent for its place as a time capsule of the popular audience it was made for. These realizations have solidified not only my love and admiration for this film, but influenced how I have come to react to cinema as an art form; how I watch movies. There is a keen sincerity I detect every time I watch *Gojira* (and frankly most of Ishiro Honda's films that speak to me). It is a similar sincerity I find attractive in most genre films, particularly horror. With the pretensions that can fall away from an already stigmatized genre, the best filmmakers can use it to really get to the core of what makes them afraid or anxious. There is something comforting in that, even if they want to share those anxieties with an audience. And there is something else to think about too.

To my mind, the horror genre can be so many different things. What is often regarded as narrow, or base, or trash (and can certainly even proudly be all of those things at times), can also be an honest reflection of the most fundamental aspects of who we are and what we feel. Horror as escapism can elicit a flight response from the problems of the real world. We can watch a fun horror movie to relish in its absurdity and get away from it all. Horror as expression can elicit, rather, a fight response—a chance to face head on the very fears many of us would rather turn away from. It can be simultaneously literal and allegorical, rational and irrational, follow linear narrative structure or meander through emotional images and sounds like a fever dream. The original Japanese *Gojira* is all of these things. It hearkens back to monster classics like *King Kong* or *The Beast from 20,000 Fathoms*, which producer Tanaka and effects maestro Tsuburaya were avowed fans of, but the need to express the present and acute anxieties of nuclear annihilation that were shared by an entire nation, and indeed an entire world, is what makes *Gojira* so much more.

It is for these reasons that *Gojira*, a film that single-handedly transformed the Japanese entertainment industry, has transcended one film to become a pop cultural icon that has lasted for over 60 years. Almost 30 films, multiple cartoons, comics, and video games, uncountable scores of toys and other memorabilia later, and the name Godzilla has become as recognizable as Elvis. He has his own Hollywood star. The ending "zilla" has even become a suffix to make anything seem monstrous or bigger than life. Dogzilla. Carzilla. Bridezilla. Despite this international recognition, the full original Japanese version didn't see an official release in the United States until a restoration and theatrical run on its fiftieth anniversary in 2004. Finally, it is getting its due recognition as a significant film, with a wonderful Criterion Blu-ray edition and presentations by world renowned film historians at notable events. With proper context, people are finally seeing beyond some of their preconceived notions of what Godzilla was at this time to something grander. The types of fears that Godzilla represents in this film are not only resonant, but they are shared across cultures. Films like this can help us to relate to and understand one another on a primal level, and really, what better conceit than that can any art hope to achieve?

PREDATOR

BY
HANK BRAXTAN

Snake Outta Compton, Unnatural,
Chemical Peel, Freddy VS Ghostbusters
Twitter: @BraxtanFilm

L et's get this out of the way: *Predator* absolutely qualifies as a horror film, and I don't think most fans would find that statement outlandish. The film boasts a huge body count (even if you take away the guerilla camp, which technically wasn't killed by the title character), the Predator kills more people than Krueger, Myers, or Voorhees get in a typical outing. Hell, if Jason had a shoulder mounted plasma cannon and swapped his creepy forest setting for a spicy jungle, he'd be right at home.

I was in second grade when *Predator* hit home video, and I remember going to quite a few video stores with my mom to find this sucker on VHS, but it was always checked out. New releases used to be a big deal, and a video store in my little town might get two copies of a popular film if we were lucky. For those who didn't grow up in the 80s, VHS used to dominate the home entertainment landscape. You used to have to find a copy of a film by leaving your house, going to a store dedicated to renting (or selling if you were really rich), finding a copy, and hoping when you got it home it hadn't been rewound too many times or damaged. But I digress…let's get to the meat of this thing.

I'll be hone, I barely remember watching the movie the first time. I'll put it into perspective: there was no internet, my nearest neighbor lived at least a half-mile away, and everything I knew about pop culture I learned from the other kids at school. I had no idea what *Predator* was about, so as it unfolded, I was as confused as the main characters, who found themselves stalked by an unseen enemy (to be fair, I probably would have thought it was two or three men out there at the most, not some fuckin' lizard).

What is that blurry thing that just killed that guy? He's dead, right?

Whoa, skinless bodies!

"Stick around!" Oh man, that's great.

Holy shit that big guy's chest muscles just exploded!

"If it bleeds, we can kill it!"

After roughly 80 minutes of cinema mastery, with all of Ahnuld's friends dead, I finally got to see it—movie monster that was such an inspired work of art that it would burn itself into my soul and guide at least some part of my being for the rest of my life. The Predator decloaked and revealed one of the greatest monster designs in cinema history.

I fell in love with what I saw. Like, for real in love. Obsessed. There was something truly special about the design that launched this beast from simple movie monster to pop culture phenom. The unmasked monster rivaled *Alien*, and the mystique, functionality, and raw power of its arsenal put it on the level of lightsabers and proton packs (and probably inspired Tesla Motors). My life had new purpose. I immediately started drawing the titular creature from the best of my recollection. (Hey, it was better than paying attention in school!) I saw no problem with this (and neither did my mom), but to kids around me (especially their parents), this obsession made me… not an ideal playmate for their perfect, *Star Wars*-loving kids. Not that there's anything wrong with *Star Wars*, mind you. I had been there, too. But this was different…this was cooler. This was gory and violent and rated R…and that meant something to children of the '80s.

I rented the film time and time again. I watched the kills in slow motion, staring into the grainy, analog VHS footage, dissecting each piece of the lore, trying to learn more about this monster. I had questions, and the answers were layered into this interlaced magnetic signal blasting into my eyeballs from my 25-inch CRT television monitor. Why did the Predator's laser blow off Dillon's arm, but Arnold took the same blast in stride, and still had the energy to yell "Get to the chopper"? Obviously, the CIA had Dillon pushing too many pencils and his puny little biceps couldn't handle the Predator's laser blast in the same manner Dutch's superior body could. This was an acceptable answer to me for years. Until the film came out on DVD, then I had the power to watch scenes frame by frame! Finally, I would…ahem…decloak this mystery. Upon closer inspection, Arnold wasn't hit by the ball of heated plasma at all…the blast instead hit his M16 assault rifle! Brilliant! This director is going places.

As a film, it works better than it has any right to do so—it's one of those times when shit just falls into place. The location was great, the cast was completely epic, and the music was on point! Then there were the little things that added up to greatness—the helicopters, the muscles, the guns, the badassery. Any one of these things would have been enough for most 80s films, but putting it all into one movie? *Predator* was groundbreaking. Full stop.

After a couple years of my unapologetic fanaticism, this film pushed me to the idea that would guide my eventual career: I was going to make a sequel to *Predator*. And why not? After many playground discussions, I had determined that my friends and I had enough collective knowledge on the subject to concoct a worthwhile follow-up. One of my friends even had a VHS camcorder! I started putting it all together: my elementary school was located next to a small wooded canyon that would serve as the perfect location for our jungle. I devised a way to launch bottle rockets as the Predator's laser weapon, and crafted a pretty sweet set of Predator armor made out of paper plates and aluminum foil. We were ready to rock.

That's when I learned my first lesson about Hollywood (and filmmaking in general): Someone beat you to it. Just before we were to start filming, I learned the bittersweet truth that Hollywood was making a *Predator 2*. So the film idea went out the window. The passion for filmmaking however—that was here to stay.

The next time you look at some silly movie with an allegedly thin plot that may involve an elite special forces unit taking on an intergalactic hunter (or the like) and you think it's low brow, remember: it's art. It may inspire some little kid somewhere to discover their passion for their own imagination. And on a final note…my *Predator* sequel totally would have been better than either *AvP* film.

Totally.

THE RETURN OF THE LIVING DEAD

BY
CHRISTOPHER M. JIMENEZ

Writer/Producer/Director
Sinful Celluloid, Danzig: Last Ride, Hellevator Man,
Scare The Devil, Mr. Black
SinfulCelluloid.com

"No one understands me, you know that?
I fucking bust my ass for you guys and what do I get?
You're spooky. Fuck you man, fuck you all!"

In 1985, I was discovering my love for zombies and my attachment to the punk rock movement that was taking over Los Angeles. Walking down the streets of Hollywood, I came to a theater showing a new zombie film and the poster caught my eye. A leather clad, mohawk-headed zombie standing by a tombstone with a big breasted zombie to his left. At the bottom of the poster was a flier for the soundtrack featuring The Cramps, The Damned, and T.S.O.L. Wow, I was in. I grabbed my popcorn and Coke and grabbed a seat. After watching *The Return of the Living Dead*, I have never been the same.

Opening up with a warning that what we are about to see is based on actual fact; we are introduced to warehouse owner Burt Wilson, his manager Frank, and his new employee Freddy. Burt leaves for the evening, but Frank wants to stick around for an hour and finish up some stuff before the long Fourth of July weekend. Freddy also stays to orientate himself with his new job.

Meanwhile, out in town, Freddy's friends are walking down the street, trying to figure out what to do that night. The group is made up of various punk types: Scuz (mohawk and trench coat), Trash (dyed red hair, fishnets, outrageous eye makeup and face paint), Spider (sporting a Jheri curl, camouflage pants, and combat boots), Chuck (new waver in an oversized suit and tie), Casey (wearing a blue "stray cats" style pompadour), and Freddy's girlfriend, Tina (kind of the good girl of the group). They decide to pick up Freddy from work because he always knows where to party and begrudgingly ask their fringe friend Suicide for a ride. He freaks them out, but he does have a car.

Back at the warehouse, Freddy is reading a medical manual while Frank does paperwork. Frank, during the course of conversation, brings up the film *Night of the Living Dead*, informing Freddy that not only was it based on a true case, but that they had some of the bodies down in the basement.

Freddy is shown the body of a corpse. Worried, he says to Frank, "These things don't leak, right?" To which, Frank assures him they don't and smacks the side of the canister, inadvertently releasing the toxic Trioxin gas!

They awake after some time to find that the gas has filled the warehouse and things are coming back to life. At the cemetery across the street, Suicide and the gang are killing time till Freddy gets off. Through some errors in judgment, the gas ends up all over the cemetery and no one is safe, not even from each other.

The Return of the Living Dead may be the second most influential zombie film ever made. Now I realize that is a bold statement but there are two traits that were given to these zombies that have endured over the years like no other.

First of all, (and I know this may come as a shock to all the *28 Days Later* devotees out there), *ROTLD* is the first film to feature running zombies as a staple. We have had them a lot in the past few years, but it started with this film. Note: I am aware of the child zombies in *Dawn Of The Dead*, but they are only seen for a moment.

Second. Look at all the zombie shirts, newspaper comics, appearances in cartoons, and so forth. What do zombies say and eat? Most people will say "Brainsssss!" Yes, this was also a creation of writer/director Dan O'Bannon, the man that also created *Alien*.

Got it? Now we can move on. On top of these changes, the film also features genre characters that feel real because it doesn't focus on their interest. I'll explain.

Punk rockers, metal heads, tattoo enthusiasts, hell, even gangsters are what I call genre guys. They have a shtick, so to speak, that represents who they are. Unfortunately, in '80s films, these characters were often parodies rather than "real" people. They were, more times than not, portrayed as goofy, violent or dim witted, rather than just being people with different musical and political agendas. O'Bannon was interested in the subculture and put them in the film as just being people in a jam, nothing more or less. These characters never feel false or forced and that is a rare thing, even today. There was even the one black guy in the group (just like me).

Another interesting ingredient is the soundtrack. The *Return of the Living Dead* soundtrack is one of the most enduring horror soundtracks ever produced, and one of only two 1980s era horror soundtracks still commonly found. One reason is that it features all original music by the biggest bands in the genre, The Cramps, The Damned, 45 Grave, T.S.O.L. and The Flesh Eaters. Most of these songs are unavailable on any other recording keeping the collectability factor high as well as because of the organic nature of Punk, it never sounds dated like so many '80s New Wave soundtracks. Trust me, you are hard-pressed to roll down the street in any city and hear someone blasting the Go-Go's (not an attack, just an observation).

During this time I had discovered a band from New Jersey in *Thrasher Magazine* who would become the unofficial epitome of the soundtrack, The Misfits. Though not featured on the soundtrack, the "ghoul rock" band sang songs and created visuals that fit into the framework of the film and further solidified the connection between the music and the film that had taken over my life.

Note: in 1987, Caliber Comics (who would go on to introduce *The Crow* to comics fans in 1989) released a comic entitled *Deadworld*. The story of young adults battling a motorcycle riding leather clad undead biker in zombie apocalypse was steeped in imagery that invoked both the punk rock esthetic and feel and texture of *The Return of the Living Dead*. I would often listen to the soundtrack to the film (along with The Misfits) when reading the latest issue.

Another area the film would affect was my expectation of horror films in regards to visuals. There are so many moments in the film that rise above anything else ever placed in a film like this. The striking moments include:

-**A graveyard full nude striptease (to music no less)** - We always have sex in our horror films but never presented so classy and well edited. It is a true music video moment that fits seamlessly into the narrative.

-**Split dogs (actually a little disturbing)** - Everybody loves dogs in film and this gag comes off as bizarre and fun. Your reaction is one of surprise until Frank (James Karen), begins to beat the undead dogs with a crutch. Once they begin to yelp, it stirs something within and you cringe. Amazing.

-**The interrogation of a half woman corpse (by half woman, I mean the top half of her body, what did you think I meant?)** never seen done so perfect as it was here, we have a conversation between half a rotten corpse and a human. From the voice acting to the swaying spinal cord, this is a horrifying marvel to behold.

-A legless zombie chasing a character on his stumps (you have to see it) – One of the most talked about scenes is when Ernie the mortician (Don Calfa) makes a run for the Paramedic Ambulance and comes across a zombie who then chases him. What makes it different? He has no legs! He is a real-life amputee and the visual he provides is unlike anything else seen in a zombie film.

These images set my expectations for horror to this day. A well put together film with people I could relate to. They listen to music I listened to. I couldn't ask for anything more.

I am often asked "why this film more than any other?" Yes, it's the union of zombies and punk rock and the relatability of the characters, but there was something even more personal going on that I didn't realize right away.

Whether it's the cemetery scene or Suicide driving around, it all seemed familiar, like a place I had been to. Well, it was. *The Return of the Living Dead* was filmed in Los Angeles! I often skated by Uneeda Medical Supplies downtown while listening to the Cramps, 45 Grave or even The Misfits. It became a game to find all the locations (a challenge in the pre-internet era).

For all these reasons, the movie buried itself deep in my consciousness, and informed the way I saw horror, music, social situations, and my city around me. It solidified my love for my favorite bands, horror sub-genre, practical effects, makeup, and more. Every aspect of horror films was represented here and, it in turn, shaped my love for horror films.

There are sly in-jokes throughout, but they never slip into slapstick, nor are the zombies ever played for laughs. If you like zombie films and have yet to see this one; you are in for a treat. If you are new to zombie films this is a great place to jump on board and catch up. It was the perfect film at the perfect time for me. It brought together two different worlds in a way that created a perfect storm. A world that has informed all of my art and the very way I see the world. Who knows, maybe after you see it, you'll be the one rolling down the street blasting the soundtrack for all to hear. No one has to understand us. We understand each other and it's not spooky at all.

CREEPSHOW
BY
DAVE PARKER

Writer/Director/Editor
The Dead Hate the Living, The Hills Run Red,
It Watches, Tales of Halloween: Sweet Tooth
Twitter: @DaveParker666

OCTOBER 1982 - PARKER FAMILY LIVING ROOM - NIGHT

A young Dave Parker sits in front of a 24" Zenith
Television, watching the trailer to Creepshow for
the first time. "The most fun you'll ever have being scared!" the narrator croaked, as the trailer
ended. I sat transfixed, turned to my dad sitting
in his recliner, and exclaimed, "We are going to
see that!"

I was kind of surprised by my own declaration. You see, from
my earliest memories I was drawn to monsters, and had
this almost primal interest in spooky stuff - dinosaurs, *King
Kong, Godzilla*, the Universal Monsters, *Famous Monsters of*

Filmland, but I was absolutely terrified of modern horror.

I remember the first time I tried to watch *Halloween* when it aired on television in 1980. I made it through the opening credits, and then left the room. The music scared me too much. Even trailers for the new crop of modern horror films like *Friday the 13th* scared me to the point of nightmares.

I had seen some "modern horror" movies by that time:

Carrie: I remember watching it with my family, and when that hand came flying out of the grave, we all hit the ceiling.

Invasion of the Body Snatchers (1978): the ending still haunts me.

Jaws 2: I was too young to see the original *Jaws*, and still hadn't, but begged to go to this one, swept up in *Jaws*-mania without knowing how terrifying it actually was. I wouldn't go swimming in our pool for a year, and I still won't go in the ocean.

I had what would be called a "vivid" or "overactive" imagination, and for some reason all the scenarios that played through my mind did not end well for me. Or…I guess you could say I was a pussy.

But for some reason when I saw that trailer for *Creepshow*, something inside made me grow a pair of balls. I was determined to see this movie…in a theater…opening night.

◆

NOVEMBER 12, 1982 - MERILL'S THEATER 6 - NIGHT

Dave and his dad watch the first screening of Creep-show opening night in a six-plex movie theater in Burlington, Vermont.

The Warner Bros. logo comes on - red and black. Eerie string music fades in. A piano sting brings the first image on screen...

...120mins later.

I walked out a different kid.

It seems funny now that this colorful, goofy, yes creepy, but also quaint movie made such an impact on me. Funny because, it wasn't *The Exorcist, Psycho, The Shining, The Texas Chain Saw Massacre* or even *Night of the Living Dead*! It wasn't trying to damage your psyche, or make you question why you are here.

It was Stephen King and George A. Romero sitting in the back of the theater, giggling their asses off as people jumped, screamed, shouted and gasped at what they had made. It wasn't subtle. This was in your face, spook house at the local fair times 100!!! A roller coaster ride of genuine thrills and chills with just enough Tom Savini gore and creatures to make it all slide down like fine scotch.

From the very opening when Tom Atkins punishes his son for reading "this worthless piece of shit" comic book, I felt kinship. Young Billy's bedroom was similar to mine, and I had many of the same toys. It could have been me. What I always wondered, later on in life, is how could the dad get so upset about the comic book, when he and his wife had obviously bought Billy all this other monster stuff that filled his room? That's not the point, of course. You aren't meant to read too deep into it, just strap in and enjoy the ride.

The moment that "The Creep" showed up, with his echoing cackle, framed by a full moon outside of Billy's window, I was hooked. When the lightning struck and he turned into animation, I was transported into a living comic book. I had never seen anything so cool in my life. Okay, maybe I was a little sheltered then, but damn, I still think that moment is some really killer shit.

For the next two hours, I sat glued to my seat, letting the wave of lurid, colored celluloid envelope me. I leapt out of said seat when Nathan Grantham's rotted hand came smashing out of the grave. Peeked through my hands as that vengeful corpse declared, "I want my cake!" and then ferociously snapped Aunt Sylvia's head backwards. Laughed at poor Jordy Verrill's abysmal luck. Held my breath as Gaylen Ross and (a then unknown) Ted Danson gasped their last as the tide rolled in. Freaked the fuck out as Fritz Weaver and some lowly janitor hammered open The Crate, unleashing a flurry of teeth and claws that I would come to know later, and very affectionately, as Fluffy. And almost gagged, watching as a foul-mouthed Upson Pratt fought a war against a horde of cockroaches that he was doomed to lose.

These five jolting tales of terror exploded every neuron of my imagination. This was my first drug experience. It was total horror euphoria. I'm not ashamed to admit that at the time, each story worked like gangbusters on me. I was scared and had nightmares after, but I couldn't get the movie out of my mind. It was like a starving person being presented with a five-course meal. I had finally tasted the forbidden fruit, and now I was ravenous.

The camera angles, exaggerated lighting, the comic styled frames, the special effects, and music, hit me like a Mack Truck. I became conscious of actual cinematic techniques such as lighting, angles, design, and editing. Like I said before, it wasn't subtle, but I hadn't been paying attention.

A quick detour - many years later I would be at a lecture given by George A. Romero, at the Director's Guild of America, where he talked and showed clips from his favorite movies. His favorite, and the one that he sighted as awakening him to movies and their techniques, was the Powell and Pressburger film, *Tales of Hoffmann* - a vivid Technicolor adaption of the famous ballet. It too had exaggerated lighting, angles, and was, some would say, similarly overdramatic. Seeing the clips from the film that Romero showed, it made me feel like a kindred spirit in that he too was affected by something that showed the power of cinema so overtly and even at times, garishly.

I knew as soon as The Creep, again animated, pulled the cover of *Creepshow* Issue 2 back, the candle blew out, and the credits rolled, that I wanted to do what these guys did. I couldn't get this movie, and its moments, out of my mind. But besides knowing of Stephen King, I had no idea who George A. Romero, or pretty much anyone else involved in the movie except for some of the actors, were.

That soon changed, as one day, by accident or by fate, I stumbled upon a comic book shop in the city. Before that, I didn't even know there were such things as comic book stores. I just got comics at the local mom and pop stores that were in my small town. It was at this shop that I found and immediately bought my first issue of *Fangoria Magazine*. It was The Bloody Best of *Fangoria* #2. Inside were stories on *Creepshow*, its director George A. Romero, and special effects wizard Tom Savini. This putrid periodical had articles about how movies were made, and about who made them. Knowledge was in my tightly grasped hands. Another rabbit hole had opened in front of me, and I dove down into an abyss that I still exist in today.

From there, it was all over. This was the early '80s. The home video boom was just starting, and pretty soon our family had our own VCR. Life then on became a constant barrage of horror movies, books, and magazines. I wasn't just delighting in all the carnage that was splattering all over my TV, but I was studying and learning, and my professors were Romero, Savini, Carpenter, Craven, Hooper, along with a multitude of other directors, writers and artists working in every genre.

I fell in love with movies, and I still love them, and that love is in very large part due to *Creepshow* and George A. Romero. The effect that this movie had on me was instant, powerful and life changing. Since that first viewing in that darkened theater in Vermont, I've watched it countless times. I can practically recite it line for line as it plays along. I love every single frame of it.

I'm not saying that this is healthy at all. Horror is an addiction, as is wanting to make movies, and trust me, you will pay the price for it. But, for better or worse, *Creepshow* and George A. Romero showed me a path that I chose to follow.

I've gotten to make movies, and in all of them I can see the shades of that film and the man in them. Either consciously or subconsciously, I've tried, with varying degrees of success, to honor, celebrate and recreate the feeling I got when I was just an impressionable kid sitting in that theater. I will continue to strive for that with each movie I make, regardless of whatever genre I work in.

Sadly, I am writing this piece just days after George A. Romero passed away. I'm devastated, to say the least. He opened up an entire world to me. Through his films, the documentaries about his films that I have been fortunate to work on, his collaborators that I became friends with, and my far too few interactions with the man himself, he has been a constant in my life, and a huge inspiration.

His loss is immeasurable. His influence incalculable. His impact undeniable.

Thank you George for everything that I have and will do. Your spirit lives within so many of us, as fans, as filmmakers, and as people. You will be missed, but you truly will live forever, like the living dead you created, in our hearts, minds, and spirits.

And *Creepshow* is still the most fun I've ever had being scared.

ALIEN
BY
ARIELLE BRACHFELD

Actor/Producer
Snake Outta Compton,
Chemical Peel, Los Angeles Overnight
Facebook: @ActressArielleBrachfeld
Twitter: @ABrachfeld

I wasn't always a horror film fan. Anything scarier than the kid's show *Are You Afraid of the Dark?* was too intense for me. I couldn't open my brother's awesome collection of *Goosebumps* books because the covers were freaky. My heart would race as I stepped through the horror section at video rental stores. I'd do my best to sway the tide at sleepovers with any choice but a horror movie.

Science Fiction and Fantasy however, that was a different story. I grew up with Isaac Asimov, Ray Bradbury, J.R.R. Tolkien, Frank Herbert, *Star Trek*, and too many more to count. I guess that's why *Alien* was the perfect gateway drug to horror films in the first place. It had my favorite elements of Sci-Fi;

space travel, production design and atmosphere that swallows you whole, a sense of mystery that hangs over every corner, a true reality to the story, amazing characters, and just the right amount of humor. It made the horror elements, the jumps, the gore, the creature effects, and the sense of dread, palatable in such a way as to sneak by my delicate, horrormovie-phobic tendencies. I was so caught up in the world the filmmakers created and so invested in Ripley, that I was carried along with the story without once covering my ears or closing my eyes during the scary parts.

There is something so special about watching good movies. You can fall into their world and get lost. You escape into whatever universe that the movie creates. It's a necessary piece for all good films. You need to create a whole universe for this fictional story to take place in order to have all the pieces fit. That starts with story and characters. It needs the right cinematography and production design. The right editing, score, and sound design. Every piece needs to fit for it to truly be an immersive experience and for the audience to get so swallowed up by watching it that they forget about the rest of the world. There's a magic in that type of storytelling that hits us on a primal level. It's one of the best experiences I think we're capable of as human beings.

With *Alien*, I got lost in this brand new world. There was no other registered sensory input, just the magic of being completely immersed in this story. No distractions, no recognition of myself watching the movie. I was totally lost in the story. That's how I first fell in love with the film. But, it was only after I became a filmmaker myself that I realized how much Alien affected me.

When I started acting in horror movies, I was struck by how great the female roles tended to be. The leads had full emotional arcs, they fought for their survival, they weren't the one dimensional "girl next door" who's just there to be something the male lead attains. They drove the story. They handled weapons, confronted major antagonists, and more often than not, had some action hero elements not usually seen outside of genre films. These characters were badass! Ripley is my golden standard of badass final girls, and frankly, I hope to one day have a similar role. I found that my own real-life strength was boosted whenever I got to play a female lead or final girl in a horror movie. There's just something so empowering about getting to play a character that overcomes such adversity.

As I began to produce more, I was also able to appreciate what technical craftsmanship went into making a movie like *Alien*. The production design is perfect. It feels like you can taste the air on the Nostromo. You feel the hum of the hull. The special effects and creature design are flawless. It's grounded in reality and it makes it all the more terrifying because it could be real. The sound design, the score, the cinematography; they elevate the film to a masterpiece.

The artistry behind *Alien* allowed me to see how horror elevates concepts. It's the only genre that can be used to probe such a variety of dark facets in human nature. It is one of the best blank canvasses to discuss themes of character and psychology. To explore our very nature. Why, at the end of the day, we can't just save ourselves. We have to save the cat.

ALIENS
BY
CALDER GREENWOOD

Production Designer/FX Artist/
Monster & Puppet Performer
Harbinger Down, Swiss Army Man,
Nosferatu, Perfect, Kuso
Instagram: @CalderGreenwood

First off, I feel the need to defend this movie as a horror movie. I'm sure for some of you, your inner dialogue right now is: "THAT DOESN'T COUNT". *Part 1* is certainly more horror whereas *Part 2* is more action, but both are certainly horrific. Yes, it's sci-fi, but there are plenty of sci-fi movies that skew more towards horror as a theme than just science fiction (*Event Horizon, Nightflyers,* even *Jason X*). So if I may move forward, let me elaborate on why.

I first saw *Aliens* at an age so young that I can't pinpoint it exactly. I remember seeing *The Ewok Adventure* at my old house before we moved, so I must have been four. I remember seeing *Poltergeist* in the new house, and that night my bedroom door creaked open for no reason. After screaming as loud as my lungs could manage and my mother saving me, the bedroom closet remained barricaded for the next three years. So I'll guess that was ages five to eight. I remember seeing *Predator* at my friend's sleepover party after watching *Wrestlemania III* (the one where Hulk Hogan body slams Andre the Giant). That was '87, so I would have been eight. Now here's the weird part about *Aliens*. The first memory I have of it that I can pinpoint is not seeing it, but being asked if I had seen it. I was 10 or so. And indeed, I remembered, that was the one where a mouth-monster rips through someone's chest. I vividly remember the image, yet my adolescent mind, incapable of processing what I was seeing, equated it to what looked like an albino alligator mouth, protruding through someone from behind. I can still picture that image - a long row of teeth, opening and closing, the rest of the beast obscured, the unfortunate victim of the creature flailing. So yes, I had seen it.

The person asking the question, one of my dad's friends, informed me that no, that's not what happened. Not quite like that anyway. So here I was, confused and 10-years-old, knowing I had witnessed the movie, I was in the room when it was playing, but maybe no, I hadn't really SEEN it. Yet that albino alligator mouth was so vivid. This was circa '89, when *Batman* was in the theater and home video was in its heyday. I had a new mission: to track down a copy of *Aliens*.

Without much effort, I eventually found it, watched the scene in question, and realized I had a much different impression of what I had seen. The chestburster was clear now, not an albino alligator with a long row of teeth but, well, a chestburster. The rest of the movie played out, had me on the edge of my seat, and in the end, didn't fill me with fear the way *Poltergeist* had, but instead a sense of awe - how did they do that? I was more preoccupied with the aliens, the facehugger, and the queen, as being marvels of cinematic wizardry, more so than just nightmare fuel.

Cut to 30 years later, I've worked with a lot of the crew

who made that movie and the subsequent sequels, including Alec Gillis and Tom Woodruff Jr. of Studio ADI, Stephen Norrington (he made the facehugger armatures), Robert Skotak (miniatures), Pat McClung (he donned the suit for the six-foot bedroom poster - I was lucky enough to own that), and Lance "Not bad for a human" Henriksen. The magic of movies and creatures and special effects has stayed with me, as clear as that image of the albino alligator.

THE TEXAS CHAIN SAW MASSACRE

BY
CLINT CARNEY

Artist/Musician/Filmmaker
Dry Blood, SYSTEM SYN
Facebook/Patreon: @ClintCarney
Instagram: @SystemSyn

As far back as I can remember, I've been in love with horror. The genre has always been in my life, and a huge part of who I am as an artist, musician, filmmaker, and person. My wife shares a love of the macabre as well, which is one of many reasons that we make a great team. I'm writing this from my home office; a room filled with horror art, movie props, FX heads, and real human skulls. Of course, if you walk into any other room in our apartment, you'd still be surrounded by other, equally horrific items. The works of many authors, artists, filmmakers, and other creative types have influenced me over the years, but when I trace back to the beginning of my horror obsession, I keep finding Tobe Hooper's *The Texas Chain Saw Massacre* at the heart of it all.

My uncle, William Michael Carney, was a horror author, and my best friend from the time I was a kid, through till his death in 2001. He was the first kindred spirit in horror that I knew, and since I grew up with him in my life, I never thought of horror as an outsider genre. It was just a part of life. Uncle Bill (or Unk, as my siblings and I called him) had a fantastic collection of films on CED (Capacitance Electronic Disc… look it up, kids) and VHS. His condo in Canoga Park, California is where I first saw just about every film that shaped my life; *Star Wars*, *Jaws*, *Alien*, and of course, *The Texas Chain Saw Massacre*. You have to understand; I wasn't terrorized by horror films. They weren't forced upon me. I simply and wholeheartedly fucking loved them. At six years old, when I saw that beautifully painted VHS box art of a man wearing a human skin mask, running at me with a chain saw, I knew this was something that I had to see. In my uncle's defense, he said I was too young to watch the movie. It took several more visits and a whole lot of begging, but he eventually relented, and my life was forever altered…for the better, I truly believe.

A black screen. Yellow text crawls up from the bottom, as John Larroquette's somber voice narrates. Rough translation of this text: You are about to watch something really fucked-up. Such a simple and perfect setup for a film, and everything that comes after does not disappoint. I'm not going to give you a play-by-play rehash of the entire film, but I would like to talk about a couple key points in *Chain Saw* that really hit you right in the gut. It is my hope that if you are reading this, there is a one-hundred percent chance that you've already watched the movie. But, if for some reason that is not the case, stop reading this right now, go watch it, and thank me later.

Leatherface (played by Gunnar Hansen) is amazing. There will be no argument there. Everyone loves Leatherface, myself included, and yes, he is the iconic figure of this film and the entire franchise. However, *Chain Saw* is so much more than a movie about a guy in a mask killing off teenagers. Sure, it has that element to it, but that's not what makes the film. *Chain*

Saw is scary, but also genuinely creepy. This film makes you uncomfortable when you watch it; makes you question whether or not you should be watching it. Many films have done that since, but *Chain Saw* paved the way, and did it best. This is in no small part owed to the wonderful performances of Jim Siedow as the Cook, and Edwin Neal as the Hitchhiker. Their characters are so vivid and real, while simultaneously being over-the-top psychotic, that it is hard not to think the actors are totally insane in real life. When you watch them on screen, you feel just as uncomfortable around them as the characters in the scenes do. These villains brought to life by Mr. Siedow and Mr. Neal make the horror of *Chain Saw* emotionally immersive for the audience. They brilliantly set the tone of unease, so that by the time Leatherface does pop up on screen, it's like getting punched in the stomach after getting food poisoning. And yes, that sounds bad, but I mean it as a sincere compliment.

Leatherface's first onscreen moment is one of my favorite villain reveals of all time. Kirk (played by William Vail) stumbles while walking through a doorway, just as Leatherface enters to meet him. Almost instantly, Leatherface whacks Kirk on the head with a sledgehammer. Kirk falls, and has a great moment of twitching on the ground before Leatherface issues the deathblow. He then slams shut a metal sliding door, closing the scene. There are no musical queues to tell us what is going to happen. It comes out of the blue, as a jolting moment of brutality. In about ten seconds, you know everything you need to about this character; he's massive, he wears human skin on his face, and he will kill you with zero hesitation. Simply terrifying. And that is only the beginning of the horror of *The Texas Chain Saw Massacre.*

Watching that movie at my uncle's became a ritual for me. He eventually just gave me the VHS. After a year or so of owning it, the tape stretched out so much from all the repeat viewings that I had to buy a new copy. And then another. And then the DVD. And then the Blu-ray. Then came T-shirts, masks, toys, etc. Hell, I even named one of my cats Sally, after Marilyn

Burns' character. (Her brother is named William, after my un-cle.) Though I never shared the same passion for the sequels, re-makes, and reboots, their existence is a testament to how fuck-ing great the first film was. Everyone wanted more, holding out hope that a follow-up would one day match the brilliance of the original. Well, we're still waiting. But that's okay; we can still watch Hooper's film any time we want.

The Texas Chain Saw Massacre is a great example to us all that you can make a great film without a lot of money. In fact, it can be argued that the limitations imposed by the budget are a big part of what made this film so real and disturbing. Having just completed my first feature film as a writer, producer, and actor, I now have an even deeper appreciation for what Tobe Hooper, Kim Henkel, and the rest of the talented filmmakers and cast pulled off in their debut film. I thank them all sincere-ly for bringing the beauty of horror into my life. *Chain Saw* Forever!

H.P. LOVECRAFT'S RE-ANIMATOR
BY
GRAHAM SKIPPER

Actor/Writer/Director/Producer
Sequence Break, The Mind's Eye, Re-Animator the Musical,
Beyond The Gates, Almost Human
GrahamSkipper.com
Twitter: @GrahamSkipper

"What is your favorite horror film?"

What a question! More specifically, what an impossible question. I'm a horror fan. Have been my whole life. And now, I'm lucky enough to work as a horror professional. Needless to say, I watch a lot of horror films. I like a huge variety of movies, and part of what I love about horror is just how diverse it is. Within the umbrella of horror, there are easily a dozen or more "sub-genres" that different audiences are fans of werewolves, vampires, splatter, horror-comedy, horror/sci-fi, zombies, monster movies…the list goes on.

So how do you settle on just one? I've deliberated for literally weeks on this simple question. Do I choose the one I think is the most technically perfect? The one I watch the most often? The one that got me interested in horror? The first one I saw? When I kept tumbling down the rabbit hole of what horror movie to choose, all I could think of was to say "Yooooooou baaaasssttttaaaaarrrrddd..." to the sadist that asked me.

At the end of the day, though, I think one's favorite horror film is ultimately an extremely personal decision. It says a lot about you - not just your taste in movies but also about every small detail of your life that surrounds that particular film. They define moments of your life. Often, a single movie can define who you are. For some reason, other genres don't seem to stand out to me as much as horror does in that regard. You don't hear people talking about how *Shakespeare In Love* changed the course of their life, but I've heard plenty of people say they won't go in the ocean after seeing *Jaws* as a kid.

But I digress. What is my favorite horror film? Well, seeing as how personal this question is, I decided to choose the film that has undoubtedly changed my life in the most profound way. That, of course, is Stuart Gordon's *Re-Animator*.

I was lucky enough to get to play Herbert West in Stuart Gordon's live stage adaptation of *Re-Animator the Musical*. I'll never forget the call I got from the man to play Dean Halsey in this adaption, comedy legend George Wendt (who I randomly knew): "Hey, have you ever heard of a guy named Stuart Gordon?"

Of course I had! He was the maniac behind *Re-Animator*. I'll be honest and say that before I got cast as Herbert West, *Re-Animator* had been the only Stuart Gordon film I'd seen. I was a horror fan, but about the most obscure I got was maybe *The Last House on the Left* or *Christine*. I thought I knew everything there was to know, but I would soon have my eyes blown wide open.

But I do remember seeing *Re-Animator* for the first time. I remember it was Halloween, and my friends and I had always heard that *Re-Animator* was super gory and featured naked girls, so of course we rented it. I remember my main thought throughout and at the end was, "I have truly never seen anything like this before." I'd seen a lot of violence, a lot of dead bodies acting of their own accord, a lot of mad scientists being mad...but *Re-Animator* was something else.

The thing about *Re-Animator* that makes it so special are the performances. Stuart was, by the time he made *Re-Animator*, a veteran of the theatre in Chicago, and so he took great care with casting the leads, as well as crafting their performances into something that is at times sick, twisted, deranged, funny, sweet, endearing...but always honest. He never plays it for schlock. He takes every moment of this insane ride seriously.

And he captures those performances perfectly! Long single takes, just like in theatre...relying on the actors' performances in times when the special effects wouldn't have cut it (West and Dan chasing the cat around the basement)...using theatre gags to sell the extreme bloodletting (which he'd also done on stage at the Organic Theater Company, of which he was artistic director).

Re-Animator is so much more than just splatter-ific entertainment - it's smart, every choice is well thought out and meaningful, the performances are spot on and - in some cases - truly legendary...but the really incredible thing is that even with all of that it is still splatter-ific entertainment. It's rare to find a horror film that is at once fun popcorn midnight fare as well as a character-driven story with very real thought and study put into every frame. *Re-Animator* is all of those things. It's perfect.

It also - I believe - kick-started today's obsession with H.P. Lovecraft. Although Roger Corman had made several Lovecraft-based movies well before this, Stuart made what is still the definitive Lovecraft film. He understood that where Lovecraft could not be directly adapted to the screen (which, let's face it, is almost impossible to do), you had to fill in the gaps. Most importantly, you had to have fully fleshed out characters with story arcs and you had to make it entertaining! His own

Lovecraftian follow-ups *From Beyond* and *Dagon* helped to cement Lovecraft as a horrific household name, and now you can buy plush Cthulhu stuffed animals at your local toy store. Stuart's responsible for all of that.

I'll add too that without *Re-Animator,* we may not have seen the catalogue of films that Stuart Gordon has gifted us with through the years. For my money, Stuart is the most consistently entertaining filmmaker I can think of. Every one of his movies is great, and even if they're not perfect, I'll gladly watch any one of them any day of the week. In addition to *Re-Animator*: *From Beyond, Dolls, Robot Jox, Castle Freak, Edmond, Space Truckers, Stuck, The Pit and the Pendulum, The Wonderful Ice Cream Suit, Fortress, King of the Ants, Dagon…* he even wrote *Honey, I Shrunk the Kids* and *The Dentist*! That is a serious filmography, full of movies that are all totally unique, unlike anything else out there, and most importantly fun.

I am incredibly lucky to have had Stuart as my mentor, and even more so to be able to call him my friend, but my love for his films and his artistry exploded when I went on my post-getting-cast-in-*Re-Animator*-Stuart-Gordon-movie-catch-up viewing rampage. All that unique blend of Gordon-esque thoughtful, deliberate, character-driven, ridiculous-premise entertainment. No one makes the absurd come to life better than Stuart Gordon. If - like me - you haven't taken the deep dive into Stuart's work, then if this essay has done any good at all, let it be that it makes a new Stuart Gordon fan.

I could gush about *Re-Animator* for days, so I will leave with simply saying that without this movie's existence I have no idea where I'd be today. I certainly wouldn't be making horror movies. As a friend of mine once said, "All roads lead back to Stuart Gordon," and it's completely true. Stuart loves the artistry of what he does, he stays loyal to his fellow filmmakers, and he will never stop perfecting even the smallest moment until it is exactly what it needs to be.

And *Re-Animator* started it all. What started as Stuart's attempt to revitalize the *Frankenstein* story that had been sadly underrepresented in recent films, has become an iconic horror film in its own right. It's launched countless careers and created some of the most unforgettable performances, gore gags, and singular moments in horror history.

As impossible as a question as "what is your favorite horror film" is, there's only one answer I could possibly give: *H.P. Lovecraft's Re-Animator.*

FRIDAY THE 13TH PART 2
BY
NICK PHILLIPS

Producer/Writer/Director
Sharon Tate and the Manson Murders, Pet, Spectres
Instagram: @NicholasCPhillips

L ike many of my generation, I grew up as a die-hard movie fan during the golden age of VHS and neighborhood video stores. Friday nights were spent with my brothers in our local Erol's Video, eagerly consuming every macabre title in the horror section. Box art was key in those days. The bloodier the better. Combine that with Saturday nights watching Count Gore DeVol hosting Channel 20's *Creature Feature*, and you have a steady diet consisting of the Gothic dream world of the Universal Classics from the '30s and '40s, the atomic paranoia giant monster hellscape of '50s films, the vibrant color and diaphanous seduction of the Hammer Films of the '60s, the next level storytelling and craftsmanship of the '70s classics and, of course, the pop orgy slasher franchises of the '80s.

But of all of those, the one movie I return to again and again, the film I still watch at least four or five times a year, is *Friday the 13th Part 2*.

Somewhere between the snuff film rough edges of *Last House on the Left* and *The Texas Chain Saw Massacre*; and the studio sheen of *The Exorcist* and *Alien*, there resides *Friday the 13th Part 2*. A studio franchise construct, no doubt, but it still contains the idiosyncrasies and indie edge of its immediate predecessors and obvious inspirations like *Halloween*.

Let me start by giving all due praise and affection to the original *Friday the 13th*. Conjured up in the wake of the runaway success of John Carpenter's *Halloween*, it was launched via a now famous ad in the Hollywood trade publications, an ad touting a project without financing or a script. But of course, in the end it delivered and subsequently spawned an entire cottage industry.

It was a down and dirty slasher flick, but it was also a murder mystery, with envelope pushing gore courtesy of Mr. Tom Savini. It featured a delightfully insane, late reveal antagonist in Betsy Palmer's Mrs. Vorhees (taking the job because she needed a new car), as well as one of the all time great final girls in Adrienne King's Alice. It established all of the hallmarks of the franchise – the jarring white outs, Harry Manfredini's frenetic and iconic score, the isolated rural setting, and a large dose of sex and death. (Kevin Bacon smoking a joint post coitus and getting a spear through the neck is of course a standout.)

But let's face it, what makes *Part 2* unique is that it introduced the world to the one and only Jason Vorhees. And I'm not talking about the slowly lumbering, hulking Jason who appeared on Arsenio. (Although I do love me some Kane Hodder.) No, I mean the burlap sack (and yes I know it was borrowed from *The Town That Dreaded Sundown*), shack dwelling, cornered feral man-child Jason.

The film starts by showing us the tortured post-massacre life of the first film's final girl, Alice. She's traumatized, no doubt, but at least we take comfort in the fact the she is alive-wait what??? Scratch that. Instead, we are shocked by her ice pick murder only minutes into the film. No one is safe. (The reasons for this are in dispute, but nonetheless it remains an effective punch in the face.)

After the film's patented off kilter-credit sequence, we return once again to Crystal Lake, now five years later. And this is the real Crystal Lake. The beautiful, lush Crystal Lake of Northeast America. Not the Crystal Lake of subsequent films shot everywhere from Southern California to Alabama to Georgia to Manhattan and even space (I mean a soundstage). Having grown up on the East Coast, I knew those woods. I explored those small towns and hidden lakes. Hell, even the bar they go to looks like my kind of joint. This is a fully realized world, and the first two films benefit greatly from shooting in these settings. They give the franchise so much of its feel and atmosphere. This could be my backyard, and Jason could be lurking there.

We meet our new final girl in Ginny Fields (named after the film's production designer). Played by the wonderful Amy Steel, she's a vibrant protagonist and worthy foil for Jason. Tough, smart, fun and beautiful. And yes, I had a massive crush on her. Steel later remarked that she wanted her character to be suspicious of cocky guys like Paul, almost unreachable, and to have a certain strength and power. She succeeds. The rest of our cast of characters is drawn well enough to have an identity and make an impact before being gruesomely dispatched.

And man, are there some great images in this film. The shot of Jason running across a narrow country road in front of the Sheriff's car is indelibly burned into my memory. Living in the sticks of Maryland, I had to drive roads like that everyday, and I even had the same car as the Sheriff (a 1980 Pontiac Le-Mans). This led to some tentative, freaked-out, white-knuckled driving if I let my imagination wander. This was not some supernatural being, this was a flesh and blood man out there in those woods; and an extremely dangerous one.

And let us never forget the horrific final shock of Jason

jumping through the window to grab Ginny. Yes it's a retread of the first film's shock scare, but it's still one hell of a kick in the balls. Stuntman Steve Daskewisz plays Jason for 95% of the movie and does an amazing job, literally and figuratively bleeding for his art. Hats off to The Dash for his kick ass work.

But it's Warrington Gillette who gets the money shot of flying through that window. (Note: As a kid, I received an autographed picture of Gillette in full makeup through a good friend. It has since been misplaced, I'm ashamed to say.) Wonderfully shot with two cameras in excruciating slo-mo, this sequence is so insane that even Amy Steel looks genuinely terrified, which only adds to the horror. And kudos to Carl Fullerton and his team, who took over here in place of the great Tom Savini. Working from Savini's Jason makeup model in *Part 1*, they create a grotesque, nightmare-inducing visage here. The stringy hair, the decayed teeth, the mottled flesh. They all work together to produce an image that will never be forgotten by this viewer.

It has been said that this is nothing more than Ginny's nightmare, and therefore this version of Jason is only what she thinks Jason might look like, which explains the lack of continuity in subsequent makeup. This theory makes no sense since she actually saw his face moments earlier when Paul removed Jason's mask. No, that's Jason alright, dream or no dream.

As touched upon before, there is ferocity to this Jason. He's not the hockey-mask-wearing, indestructible zombie of the later films. This Jason runs, he's angry, and he can be hurt. As Ginny mentions earlier in the bar, he's almost like a scared child. The kills are also more grounded and subdued, at least by slasher film standards. In subsequent films, Jason pretty much became the hero, and we were all too happy to see the dopey, annoying teens get taken out in increasingly cartoonish ways, although the sleeping bag head smash in *The New Blood* is still a top kill of the whole franchise.

In *Part 2*, we have Jason utilizing the simple tools at his disposal. A garrote (Crazy Ralph, we hardly knew ya), the trusty machete, the pitchfork, a spear (thanks, Ted), and a hammer (that looked like it hurt, Sheriff), among others. There are two kills which of course revolve around an ill-advised but utterly necessary late night skinny dip. The spectacle of the proud and driven Mark plummeting down the steps in his wheelchair in the rain is about as bombastic as it gets, and, even though it was lifted directly from Bava's *Twitch of the Death Nerve*, the Jeff and Sandra kabob is still pretty fantastic. But overall, these are restrained and simple kills, again grounding the film and creating more believable, tangible horror.

Of course, there are the gaffes, retcon problems, and logic holes, all of which I am willing to forgive. The biggest of course is, how the hell is Jason alive? And how did Jason locate and travel to kill Alice? Who peed under the bed, Ginny or the rat? (It's the rat. Period.) Wait, I thought Muffin was dead? And what the hell happened to Paul?

For me, *Friday the 13th Part 2* is the last great film of the franchise. It's like the amazing second season of your favorite TV show. It set the pattern in season one, perfected it in season two, but it then becomes a little too self aware and predictable, yet still enjoyable, in season three and beyond. It was now in on the joke.

Look, of course I've seen all of the other films in the franchise many, many times, and *Parts III, IV* and *VI* hold very special places in my heart. Years later, while working at Dimension Films, I had the pleasure of meeting Steve Miner. He was directing *Halloween H20* for the company, and I was just a lowly assistant at the time, but I managed to tell him how much his films meant to me. He was gracious and kind, even though I'm sure he's been hearing it for decades.

But this gritty thrill ride is the one that had the biggest impact on me. It is both utterly of its time and yet completely timeless. This film made me look twice at the woods which surrounded my childhood home, and it was also one of the films that literally made me pick up a camera. I was fortunate enough to own an early '80s shoulder mount home video camera, and I went about creating a slasher franchise of my own in which my younger brother and I devised lo-fi ways to off one another. No matter what type of film I am making, in whatever genre, deep down I'm still that kid with a video camera trying to recreate the terror of the woods around Crystal Lake.

(FINAL NOTE: Honorable Mention must go to *Jaws, Alien, The Exorcist, The Omen, The Wolfman, Frankenstein, Frankenstein Meets the Wolfman, The Bride of Frankenstein, Halloween* (and pretty much anything else John Carpenter directed), *The Texas Chain Saw Massacre, Deliverance, Rosemary's Baby,* and *Psycho,* among many, many others.)

DAY OF THE DEAD

BY
MICHAEL KLUG

Screenwriter/Film Critic/Actor
Horror Freak News & Tom Holland's Terror Time
Facebook: @Michael.Klug.98
Twitter: @Klugula
NotMyMess.com

George A. Romero's *Day of the Dead* made me cry the first time I saw it. Not because I loved the characters (which of course, I did). Not because something so sweet or wonderfully melodramatic occurred (it didn't – unless you count Bub's post-death loyalty to and love for Dr. Logan "Frankenstein").

And not because some sort of outside impetus occurred (i.e. I didn't skip from the room to grab more popcorn in the middle of the film and accidentally stub my toe, cry out in pain, thus blaming the film for this boo-boo).

No.

The film made me cry because it scared me. And it scared

me good.

My older brother has always pointed out Bernard Rose's *Candyman* as the horror film which most bothers/terrifies him, and not just on the surface – but on some sort of deeper, primal level.

Day of the Dead is the film which does that to me. I saw it when I was 12 years old (on VHS – the double feature that evening also included *Vision Quest*), and it has completely changed my life.

Fast forward to this year, and to the passing of my idol and creative inspiration – Mr. Romero. I was literally devastated by his death – with a broken heart, I sobbed. I cried. And at one point even vomited. Stress? Grief? That'd be my guess.

No joke.

And when I watched *Day of the Dead* for the umpteenth time in my life – just a few days after his death – the film made me cry again. For very different reasons.

Now…I've written extensively about my favorite horror film of all time (in fact, it's actually my favorite film of ANY kind – with the Sally Field/James Garner romantic comedy, *Murphy's Romance* holding the second place title).

But what I'd like to take a closer look at on this particular examination – is WHY it so destroyed me on that first viewing. What buttons did it push? Why were these images and these ideas and these characters so powerful as to single-handedly create a zombie fan for life?

It's an obsession folks. It truly is. And Sarah, Dr. Logan, Bub, Rhodes and the rest – as well as the big man in the big glasses behind these characters – are all to blame for this wild ride I've taken over the last 32 years!

So as Sarah and McDermott throw caution to the wind (what choice did they have?), grab that random piece of lumber, and jet off into the dark tunnels of the zombie corral – I'll go with them and attempt to discover what it is about this film – that keeps me coming back for more…

1) There's an innate fear in my brain (perhaps everyone's) about being eaten alive. I not only have a very illegitimate fear of zombie flesh-eaters (*Day of the Dead* sparked a lifelong affair with detailed and frightening zombie nightmares), I also have the very real phobia of sharks and shark attacks and being eaten by sharks. Admittedly, my shark fear probably has a lot to do with open water and the unknown (thanks first reading of the novel *Jaws*) – but the idea of being eaten by something else is at the base of this fear.

So with the gory and brilliant special effects by Savini and crew in the film – how can that fear of zombies be put to rest? Clearly the big show in the film is Rhodes' death. It's a tour-de-force of special effects ingenuity, blood-letting and long-lasting horrific images.

But if I had to choose the most disturbing death, it'd probably be Torrez (Taso Stavrakis). He's the first of the soldiers to go in the film's breathless climax, and it's pretty gnarly. As he's surrounded by the zombie horde, and they begin to tear him apart – his screaming (how can that not linger in your brain?) turns into a high-pitched squeal as his head is removed from his still spasming body. And even when the vocal chords are clearly severed and the screaming stops – his mouth is still going through the motions.

I mean, c'mon…that's just not right.

2) The underground isolation of the film's setting is certainly partially to blame for the film's power. It's no secret that the film was shot in an old limestone mine in the hills near Pittsburgh. The cast and crew were notoriously ill for a lot of the filming – day after day inhaling all of the pollutants and dust lingering in the breezes of this vast system.

But what the location does to the psyche of a young viewer like me – is immeasurable. There's no escape. There's no rest. It's sunless, damp and seemingly never-ending. What the hell is around each corner of this place? And it's depressing – seeing how these soldiers live – in bare rooms with nothing more than a cot and an impressive rack of automatic weapons.

And I think that what most makes my point is a line of dialogue from Rhodes as he ramps up his rhetoric to his men and the civilians – not long after he takes control – in light of Major Cooper's demise (now that I think of it – how did Cooper die? Was it at all suspicious? Hmmm…).

"Where does it say we have to keep those dumb-fucks next door to where we sleep? Where does it say we should do any one thing but shoot them all in the head?"

Exactly. Exactly. What kind of stress is there for these people stuck in this underground facility (aside from the isolation and depression and lack of vitamin D) – knowing that just over in that half-assed corral – there are dozens (if not hundreds) of hungry walking corpses roaming about?

Miguel (Antone DiLeo) is a perfect example of what this world does to a person. I often like to think that I'd do pretty well in a zombie apocalypse. But I know that I'd be just like Miguel. I'd maybe survive the onset – but once it all sets in – what life is now about, what can never be and that there are rotting corpses which want to eat me alive – will always keep me on edge…it's a sad state of affairs, and only those survivors with the strongest mind and best of endurance will last.

There's fear in that realization. I wouldn't last long. My mind wouldn't take it.

Which brings me to the other thing which has swept through my mind – over and over these many years. And it's not just *Day of the Dead* – but basically any zombie film. *Day of the Dead* just shows how terrible it will become and that even our "trusted" government will be of no help.

3) The breakdown of society as we know it.

Dawn of the Dead is a better example of this particular fear. *Day of the Dead* is the equally terrifying picture of what's to come when things "settle down".

I think the conversation between the soldiers and McDermott (Jarlath Conroy) is the most telling about how things will never be the same.

"The power's out in the mainland and all the shopping malls are closed."

A nice in-joke to the proceedings of *Dawn of the Dead* – but things like this, which were a stark reality, showcasing the world after this disaster – petrified me. Not that I didn't love shopping as a kid, but this fear was more than that. It's the fact that everyday things were now a fantasy, a long-ago memory. Not to mention family, friends, school. These things no longer exist and no longer matter.

Romero's zombie films have always been about the people, the survivors. And it's our suspicions, our human nature and our poor communication which truly fuck things up.

I can appreciate those grander ideas now – the consumerism run rampant in *Dawn of the Dead*, the lack of decent co-operation, sexism and racism in *Day of the Dead* – but initially, the thought that this is where we could end up, when society crumbles? It's absolutely chilling.

So those things – even if I couldn't quite understand them as a 12-year old zombie fanatic in the making – are why I so deeply adore *Day of the Dead*.

But the bottom line? *Day of the Dead* just scared me.

And now here I am – taking another look at a film which has changed my life and steered my professional career as a horror critic, a horror screenwriter and a proud horror nerd (with a specialty in bloody zombie goodness).

At a recent screening of the film – at this year's Screamfest (where the powers-that-be honored Romero with a screening of *Night of the Living Dead*, *Day of the Dead* and *Creepshow*) – I cried anew.

Did it scare me? Not so much. I've seen it over 1,000 times, folks. And that is in no way an exaggeration. I know every square inch of its score, the timing of dialogue (and how its delivered). I even know when the clown zombie appears in the hallway at the climax (pursuing Steele) – I know which direc-

tion he'll be facing when the edit happens (it's to screen-right).
So it didn't scare me, per se.

Did I cry again because George is gone? Yes. Absolutely.

But what truly made me tear up at this latest viewing? Some deeper reason was at play here.

So I think the reason I got mushy this last (excuse me, most recent) time – has to do with my genuine love for this film. I can't get enough of it. I can't not quote it daily. I have to look at it with awe and wonder – that this film so terrified me upon first viewing, that it changed the course of my life – not just my movie-watching fanaticism. I'm a fan sure, but there's more.

IT. CHANGED. MY. LIFE.

So how can I not appreciate something so bold and moving and inspiring? So many technical marvels (Romero was a tremendously gifted editor) to enjoy – again and again. Great characters, raw performances. Zombie gore and effects which stand the test of time.

And the deep-seated and inescapable fears which rise up (I'm not a kid anymore) into my throat – making me remember that first viewing. When McDermott and Sarah go into that corral with no weapons (just that two-by-four) – I closed my eyes and covered my ears.

And I cried.

What is there to take away from this essay? *Day of the Dead* makes me cry.

And with 32 years of watching this film – there are now too many reasons why.

Day of the Dead is mine – it's all mine.

Okay, not all mine – but I sometimes like to believe that Romero made this just for me. I met him on a couple of occasions. And while I'm sure I awkwardly gushed to him about what the film meant to me – I wish there were a way (even in this rambling essay) to make him (wherever he is) and everyone in the world truly understand how important this film is to me. Can anyone really "get it"?

Now if you'll excuse me, I'm going to go watch this film

again (1001 times?) and see if I can keep my eyes open once we reach the corral.

I'm sure George is somewhere out there saying, "Good luck with that. Oh, and stay scared."

Will do. Now hand me some tissues, I've got something in my eye…again.

For good measure:

Day of the Dead's most frightening image? "The Dead Walk" headline on the blowing newspaper in the film's opening sequence.

Day of the Dead's most frightening line of dialogue? When Dr. Frankenstein (Richard Liberty) spouts off a fun little bit of trivia (which happens to terrify me): "We're in the minority now. Something like 400,000 to 1, by my calculations."

BRAM STOKER'S DRACULA

BY
TAMMY SUTTON-WALKER

Visual Effects Supervisor/Producer
The Conjuring, Avatar, Final Destination 2 & 3,
Blade: Trinity, Twilight
Twitter: @Tamity
Instagram: @Tammy_Sutton

I t is impossible for me to pick my favorite horror movie. It
all depends on what mood I am in, so instead, I am taking
the easy way out and picking the horror movie that I have
watched more times than any other, *Bram Stoker's Dracula*.
This is one of my favorites and I often have had to defend my
stance on this one, so what better way than to put it in writing.

For as long as I can remember, I have always been drawn
to the spookier side of things. I grew up in an area of California
where a lot of movies were filmed. This gave me my first insight
to how movies were made and because of this, I did not scare
easily. I knew all the blood and guts were just "movie magic"
and were usually more amusing than scary. I was drawn to the

fun of darker movies and TV, and especially to vampires, in part thanks to Anne Rice.

When it came out in 1992, I watched *Bram Stoker's Dracula* for the first time at age 16. I went to the theater with friends who were bored and started making jokes and talking over the movie. I was sucked in from the very start, but my friends decided to leave. I went with them, leaving before the movie was even halfway through. A year or so later, I rented it on VHS from a grocery store and this was the true beginning of my love for the movie. I spent many of my hard-earned fast food wages on rental fees and late fees.

My reasons for liking this film have grown and evolved over time. Originally, I was drawn in by the romance of the story. I liked that Dracula had a backstory and a heartbreaking reason for why he becomes a monster. The use of silhouette and shadow puppets for Dracula's backstory is haunting, and I can picture the gruesome scene in my imagination even though we do not see this on the screen. A good portion of the story is told through the character's journals and letters, using voiceovers and visual imagery more than dialogue. I could watch without sound and still be captivated. Dracula is clearly the villain of the story, but I found myself sympathizing with him more than the human characters. After many repeat viewings, I started to notice the details of the costumes, the sets and the score. In college, I would often fall asleep watching *Dracula*; I knew the movie so well that it would not keep me awake and I would fall asleep just listening to it.

I started working in the movie industry 20 years ago, working in visual effects. This gave me a new perspective of *Dracula*. I started to appreciate more of the filmmaking aspects, the in-camera effects, the directing choices, the acting, and the editing. Even though I work in visual effects, I think the choice to use all practical effects is part of the charm. It created a look for the film that sets it apart from other films. This movie reminds me to think of practical solutions when planning scenes that require effects, or a combination of practical and digital. Gary Oldman is amazing. No one else could pull off that double-coned white wig or ridiculously long red cape without it turning comedic. His performance elevates the rest of the cast and helps me to overlook a bad accent or two. I am still in awe of the costume work. Every year, I think of going as one of the characters for Halloween and end up changing my mind because I could never do the costumes justice; I would have to make them perfect, down to every last detail. I love the choice to have Dracula's shadow have a mind of its own, as if it is trying to act out what Dracula is thinking.

Bram Stoker's Dracula is in no way a perfect movie, it certainly has its flaws. But for me, the good and the great moments outweigh the bad, and has made for many enjoyable repeat viewings for me. There are many images from this movie that have become iconic. If I hear someone mention a vampire or Dracula, I think of this version portrayed by Gary Oldman and the many faces he wears in this film. After all these years, *Bram Stoker's Dracula* is still my go-to movie to fall asleep to.

THE SIGHTING
BY
FRANK MERLE

Writer/Director
The Employer, #FromJennifer
FrankMerle.com
Twitter: @RealFrankMerle

I was a late bloomer to the social aspects of horror fandom. I'd been watching and loving horror films since fourth grade, but my relationship with them had been a secret, shared only with a few friends whose tastes I thought were as strange as my own. But after nearly twenty years of private horror film consumption, my eyes were finally opened to the wider world around me in 2008 when I attended my first horror convention. Within the hallowed halls of a Louisville conference center, I discovered the vast, enthusiastic community of which I had unknowingly been a member. I found myself surrounded by the monsters I had grown up idolizing and the friendly fans who worshipped them. It was an overwhelming, magical experience for me. During this festival of fright, at one o'clock on a

Sunday afternoon, I decided on a whim to pop into one of the several movie screenings that were playing off to one side of the convention hall. I sat in a darkened multipurpose room, with no expectations of what I was about to see. There I watched the movie that immediately became my favorite horror film. Objectively, it may not be a perfect film, but it's pretty darn close to perfect in my book, made all the better by the environment and mindset with which I first encountered it.

Eight years later, this film would finally receive a fairly quiet VOD/DVD release as *The Sighting*, with new music and ten minutes cut from its original run time. But when I saw it at one of its very first public screenings, it was called *Paper Dolls*. This decidedly non-frightening title may have been part of the reason it took so long to find distribution, but it's a sad reality of the independent film business that sometimes the best movies struggle to get discovered among all the noise, especially a low-budget one with a cast of mostly unknown talent. Apparently, during its distribution search, the title was changed from *Paper Dolls* to *Travis* before settling on *The Sighting*. As a filmmaker myself, I can relate to the challenge of trying to find a perfect title that captures the imagination and communicates the tone and plot of the film in three words or less. It's not always an easy task. While the title *Paper Dolls* makes perfect sense once you've seen the film, I support their decision to change it. Without giving too much away, it's safe to say this movie is not about paper dolls. In fact, there are no dolls of any kind. So the new title *The Sighting* is certainly more accurate, if only slightly more fear-inducing.

With the assumption that you probably haven't seen it, due to its criminally unjust lack of exposure, I will attempt to stay away from too many spoilers as I explain why I love this film so much. First of all, it's a slow-burner with plenty of character development between the protagonists, best friends on a road trip. Their banter is charming and their friendship is believable. The viewer wants to be on this road trip with them, so when night falls and bad things start to happen, it matters. This may be a very basic filmmaking concept, but it is extremely well executed here. The terror had me on the edge of my seat because the filmmakers had taken the time to make me care about the protagonists. Admittedly, some of the effect was lessened when they trimmed ten minutes off of the film (mostly from the first act) before its eventual release as *The Sighting*. But it still holds up as a carefully paced character-driven thriller, just not quite as boldly as before those cuts, which were apparently made as a compromise with the distributor. It pains me to see negative comments on this film's trailer on YouTube from haters writing something like, "so boring, turned it off after thirty minutes." Sadly, their impatience made them miss out on the emotional roller coaster and twisty plot of the film's second and third acts. It's their loss, of course, and negativity on the internet is nothing new, but it still bothers me when people prefer mindless, quick kills over smart storytelling.

Ostensibly, *The Sighting* is a Bigfoot movie. This isn't much of a spoiler, as this is revealed in the trailer, in the artwork, and in most descriptions of the film. But it's not your average Bigfoot movie, which is to say, the mythology the film creates to explain the existence of Sasquatch is remarkably fascinating, dealing with Spanish conquistadors, slaves in chains, inbreeding and ritualistic tongue removal. The original title *Paper Dolls* refers to these creatures' method of hunting. Locked-armed, ready to attack, they look vaguely like linked paper cut-outs, only life-sized and hairy. The full explanation of this mythology is ingeniously revealed in my favorite scene, a creatively animated flashback sequence at the halfway point of the film. As a gross generalization, most Bigfoot films aren't this clever, so whenever I'm describing *The Sighting*, I feel compelled to explain that it's not just a Bigfoot movie. It's so much more than that. Or maybe it isn't really a Bigfoot movie at all.

Calling *The Sighting* a Bigfoot movie might be like calling *From Dusk Till Dawn* a kidnapping movie. But I'm getting dangerously close to spoiler territory here, so I'll keep this next part cryptic. *The Sighting* has a literally mind-numbing twist.

No, I did not just misuse the word "literally." When I walked out of that first screening, my mind actually felt numb from over-thinking what I'd just seen. So much so that I wanted to see it again, right away. Like *The Sixth Sense, The Others,* or any such capable film premised on a great twist, it offers a very different experience upon a second viewing, once you know what's up. Some people interpret the ending differently than I do. Some say that it's more of an ambiguous, open-ended conclusion, rather than a twist. But to me, there's only one interpretation of the ending, and it turns a good film into a great film. But in the hope that I've piqued your interest enough for you to seek out this film for yourself, I don't want to say any more and ruin it for you. So in the words of Forrest Gump: "That's all I have to say about that."

Without knowing at the time that it would take eight long years for this film to be officially released, I contacted the filmmakers on social media right after that first (woefully under-attended) screening to let them know how much I enjoyed the film and that I couldn't wait to see it again. They kindly responded by sending me a DVD screener, so long as I promised not to share it with anyone, to which I thanked them and assured them that I would not. But I wasn't able to keep my promise. I ended up sharing it with everyone I could. I'm sure they were mostly concerned about piracy, and so I never let my bootleg disc out of my possession, but whenever I had a horror-loving friend over to my place, I'd offer to show them the best movie they'd never heard of. Inevitably, a new fan would be recruited and together we would lament this film's obscurity. But if I'm truly honest with myself, the film's low profile has been part of the fun for me. Whenever someone asks me what my favorite horror film is, I take pleasure in knowing with some certainty that they haven't seen the movie I mention. It makes me feel like the ultimate horror hipster, if that's a thing.

So when I was asked to write an essay about my favorite horror film, I had to consider whether I was ready to let everyone in on my secret. I could instead have written a scholarly deconstruction of *Halloween*, or *Scream*, or any number of canonized horror films you've probably seen. But that would have been selfish of me, to continue the injustice of keeping *The Sighting* in the dark. So I decided it was time to spread the word, to encourage everyone to see it, and maybe even help a few like-minded smart-horror fans discover a new favorite. But if you're like those YouTube commenters who think it's boring and you decide to turn it off after thirty minutes, that's perfectly fine. I realize that art is subjective, and there are plenty of faster paced horror films out there for you to enjoy. But because the smarter, deliberately thoughtful, artfully twisty films are harder to come by, it's up to those of us who enjoy them to bang the drums and let everyone else know about them when we find them. Perhaps if more of us did so, without risk of ridicule from the "it's so boring" crowd, it wouldn't take beautiful films like *The Sighting* eight years (and two title changes) to find distribution.

AN AMERICAN WEREWOLF IN LONDON

BY
JOSHUA LOU FRIEDMAN

Assistant Director/Filmmaker/Actor
Bitch Slap, Big Ass Spider, Tales of Halloween,
Lavalantula, I Spit on Your Grave III: Vengeance is Mine
Facebook: @JoshuaLouFriedman

While the summer of 1982 famously bred such beloved horror classics as *Poltergeist*, *The Thing* and *Creepshow*, I'll always remember 1981 as being the "Year of the Wolf"...and for very good reason.

At that time, I was quite literally beginning my teenage years, which also meant I was not only bursting with hormones, but had this insatiable appetite for whatever film *Fangoria* magazine (still basking in the innocence of its inaugural issues) would tell me to look out for. Among the swarm of titles swimming within that whirlpool were *Friday the 13th*, *Dead and Buried*, *Scanners* and *The Evil Dead*. However, the ones that rose to the surface for me were *The Howling, Wolfen* (both novel adaptations), and the long-in development passion project from National Lampoon's *Animal House* director John Landis, entitled *An American Werewolf In London.*

I remember hating that title upon first hearing it...today however, the mere utterance of those words spark memories of both laughter and terror spent beneath the canopy of a darkened theater. Many theaters in fact...as I ended up seeing it at least 13 times on the big screen. The grand mash-up of horror and comedy had been tried and done before...sometimes with success as in *The Raven* (1963) or *The Fearless Vampire Killers* (1967), while other times not so much as with 1973's *Arnold* (if you've never even heard of that last one, the defense rests). The formula proved not only successful in Landis' case, but emerged as an inspired one, as 90% of any original work I've ever committed to paper would adopt this two-punch of shocking thrills followed by an immediate burst of levity.

It's fair to say that (upon repeat viewings) the goose bumps still kick in the moment we hear Bobby Vinton's rendition of "Blue Moon" permeate the opening frames, thus heralding the 97 minutes of pure excitement to come. From David Kessler and Jack Goodman (respectively played by David Naughton and Griffin Dunne) trading snappy quips while trekking across the Yorkshire moors, on to Kessler's painful journey through his lycanthropic affliction, through being both delighted and disgusted every time Dunne's decomposing character would drop in to further the exposition, and finally to the final act's all-out mayhem as the beast wrecks havoc through Piccadilly Circus. Catching *An American Werewolf in London* never felt like going to a mere movie to me...it was more of a full-blown experience, as I was having a great time in a movie theater.

This power the movie had on me would cement my love for not only the genre, but for all films and filmmaking in general.

And I continued to eat it up...when not in school, my teenage years were pretty much spent in a movie theater. My first-ever paying job was in a movie theater...in fact it was that theater: the one where I first laid eyes upon *An American Were-wolf in London* a mere four years before, the General Cinema 6 in Redondo Beach, California. And it wasn't just a place of employment to me…for in my eyes, it was a church, and I was its mere disciple (spreading gospel to those who wandered off the street to catch *Out of Africa* or *Cocoon* at the bargain matinee price of $3.55).

Evidence of the film's hold on me continued to pop up over the course of my life:

-Not only would I find a way to have Van Morrison's "Moondance" play in the background during many o' romantic trysts…it even played as I walked down the aisle at my first wedding.

-When I finally began working the industry, one of my first gigs in the AD department was on a werewolf picture entitled *Big Bad Wolf,* which featured none other than David Naughton as the ill-fated Sheriff Ruben. Now, I'm usually pretty good about not getting too starstruck on set, but come on! (And yes, he's a great guy to work with).

-In 2010, I was lucky enough to co-star in a film shot in London entitled *Big Fat Gypsy Gangster.* While visiting Piccadilly Circus during our nearby night-shoot, our DP, Gary Shaw (who shot both *Moon* and *Mute* for director Duncan Jones), noted my enthusiasm for being there (and why), before leaning over and admitting he started out as a camera assistant on *An American Werewolf in London* in the early days of his career. He proceeded to give me an on-the-spot firsthand tour of what was where and how it was shot, upon which, I happily gobbled up every anecdote after precious anecdote.

And finally…

-Getting to write this very piece for the book you're currently holding in your hot little hand!

Now that's a great way to cap off a love affair I've had with a film ever since 1981...which coupled with *The Howling* and (especially) *Wolfen*, will forever in my eyes be considered the "Year of the Wolf".

HALLOWEEN
BY
MICHAEL GINGOLD

Writer/Editor/Screenwriter/Disc Content Creator
Fangoria, Rue Morgue, Shark Movie Mania,
The Frightfest Guide to Monster Movies
Facebook: @MichaelGingold12

All through my preteen years, I couldn't handle horror films. I was that kid who was freaked out by scary stuff. Forget watching through my fingers; I would actually stand while viewing genre flicks on TV, just in case they got to be too much and I had to run from the room. I was a big fan of *Godzilla* and similar monster movies, but the harder-core stuff—even the ones that were rated PG—was too intimidating. I did want to see *Jaws* when it first hit theaters just because I was so into sharks at the time, though the "May be too intense for younger children" note on the ads forestalled that possibility.

Things began to change around the time I turned 12. I went to see *Invasion of the Body Snatchers* with my family and made it through unscathed (though today, I'm stunned it got away with a PG rating). Through the following spring and summer, I began getting curious about horror, and seeing a few of the R-rated examples—like *Phantasm* and *Alien*—along with *Jaws*, finally. They all had the desired effect, and I hid my eyes during *Phantasm*'s silver sphere scene and *Alien*'s chestburster. Still, I began not only getting comfortable with being frightened by film, but enjoying the sensation—the natural high it created. My intrigue was fueled by a cover story in *Newsweek* called "Hollywood's Scary Summer," and the emergence of a new magazine called *Fangoria* (which featured my old friend Godzilla on the front of its first issue). And later in 1979, I saw the movie that made me love being scared.

I was vaguely familiar with John Carpenter's *Halloween*, having seen a television ad or two when it first opened in October 1978. At that time, a newspaper-workers' strike had shut down *The New York Times*, the paper in our household, so I didn't read much about the movie then; in fact, I read more about it during a family vacation to England in the summer of '79, when it had opened in the UK to lots of positive attention. Back then, however, before the video market took over, popular movies were rereleased all the time within a year or so of their initial openings, and so it was with *Halloween*, which returned to theaters in October '79. That's when I first saw it, and I didn't know what hit me.

Never mind the now-classic opening single-take shot from young Michael Myers' point of view; the damn *music* frightened me before the film proper even started. Carpenter's simple but chilling 5/4-time theme had my hackles raised within the first minute, and the movie had me in its grip from then on. I don't recall if I screamed out loud, but my grandmother, who took me to the movie (my parents just weren't into the horror stuff), was genuinely concerned afterward at how frightened I had been.

She needn't have worried. I had indeed been scared half to death by *Halloween*, more than by anything I'd ever watched before, and yet I had found it exhilarating. It was a huge change in the way I experienced movies. A year before, I had barely been able to take a made-for-TV schlocker like *Devil Dog: The Hound of Hell*; now, a movie that was originally advertised with the tagline "When were you last scared out of your wits by a movie?" had completely lived up to that promise—and I enjoyed the hell out of it. (The reissue ads, conversely, were stocked with laudatory quotes from critics. Contrary to popular belief, *Halloween* attracted a number of positive reviews from the start; one of my favorite excerpts—I can't recall the source now—was "It'll scare the seeds out of your pumpkin.")

Part of the reason *Halloween* was so effective was that it literally got me where I lived. I grew up in exactly the kind of suburban town where Michael comes home to do his dirty work, and what makes the scenes between his prologue slaying of his sister and his All Hallows' Eve rampage work so well is how ordinary, and thus relatable, they are. There's nothing special about Jamie Lee Curtis' Laurie and her friends, nor are they the hopped-up sex and party monsters of so many subsequent slasher films; they're just typical teenage girls with typical teenage concerns. Producer and co-scripter Debra Hill reportedly wrote most of the heroines' dialogue, and demonstrated a remarkable skill at capturing the tone and tenor with which young women conversed—not to mention that Lynda's (P.J. Soles) favorite expression "totally" anticipated Frank and Moon Zappa's hit song "Valley Girl" by four years.

Once we've gotten to know our central trio, along with young Tommy (Brian Andrews), whose dread of *Halloween* and "the bogeyman" helps amplify our own, Carpenter tightens the screws with merciless precision, demonstrating a remarkable handle on composition, framing and pacing. Even as I was caught up in Laurie and co.'s escalating fright, *Halloween* was the first time I was aware that a movie was *directed*, and I was able to admire Carpenter's craft at the same time it was holding me in a death grip.

I became an instant Carpenter fan, eagerly anticipating

each new film from the director (I didn't have to wait long; *The Fog* debuted only five months later). I reviewed *Halloween* for my junior-high-school newspaper; one of the first pieces of criticism I ever wrote. I attempted to teach myself Carpenter's *Halloween* theme on the family piano, and almost mastered it. I read Curtis Richards' novelization and was puzzled by why the author felt it necessary to throw in the distracting backstory about Samhain (if only I knew...).

And when *Halloween II* opened in 1981, three friends and I went on Halloween night. This was back before sequels and franchise pictures had taken over the movie scene the way they have now. We weren't dutifully catching the latest entry in an established series, we were getting more *Halloween!* The entire audience was primed for it, and we all responded with screams and laughs at the right places, shouted advice to Jamie Lee Curtis and "Shut up!" when that dumb cop says something stupid during the climactic action. Some consider *Halloween II* unworthy of its predecessor, but I'll probably never be able to judge it objectively, because seeing it that first time was one of the best moviegoing experiences of my life. Part of the thrill was that we all went in costume, figuring the disguises would help our 14 and 15-year-old selves get into this R-rated movie without a parent or adult guardian, and we were right; seeing it unchaperoned was part of the excitement.

In the years since, I've seen hundreds (thousands?) of horror films, but none will ever hold the place in my heart that *Halloween* does. *Halloween* was the movie that crept into my psyche and unlocked that area where the fascination with the dark, scary and unknown resides. It transformed me from a casual fan of fright cinema to a passionate follower of the genre - just at the right time, when horror had its explosion of popularity in the very late '70s and early '80s. It was the film that I held all subsequent scare films up against. And it led me to a career in the horror field, fulfilling the dream that *Halloween* first inspired. One of my proudest achievements is the 8,000-word-plus history of the cinematic Michael Myers saga that I wrote for the booklet accompanying Shout! Factory and Anchor Bay's *Halloween: The Complete Collection* deluxe Blu-ray boxed set. (On the other hand, when I took a gig scripting a very-low-budget movie called *Halloween Night*, my attempt to honor Carpenter's legacy was completely stymied by the execution.)

I've seen *Halloween* countless times since that first viewing back in '79, and while it doesn't frighten me now like it did back then, I am still in thrall to what a relentlessly well-crafted film it is. To me, it's one of those perfect movies, one that doesn't have a wasted moment, in which all the elements click together perfectly. From the performances to the music to Dean Cundey's mobile cinematography, which draws us right into the action (though it does not, as commonly thought, take Michael's point of view at any point after his childhood prologue), every part of *Halloween* works in concert toward one goal: To terrify you, to leave you shaking when it's over, yet to make you feel elated rather than worn down. *Halloween* did that to my 12-year-old self better than any other movie has since, and that's why it remains my favorite horror movie.

VALERIE AND
HER WEEK OF WONDERS
BY
STACI LAYNE WILSON

Writer/Director/Author
Cabaret of the Dead, Psycho Therapy,
So L.A. - A Hollywood Memoir
Instagram: @StaciLayne Facebook: @StaciWilson

Through no design or intent, I happened to watch two movies back-to-back in which 13-year-old girls lost their virginity and found that the world is full of wolves, vampires and weasels. The first was a revisit to Neil Jordan's darkly lush exploration of the *Little Red Riding Hood* mythos in *The Company of Wolves*. The second is the film I'm discussing here, a vintage Czech malice in wonderland surrealist allegory called *Valerie and Her Week of Wonders*.

Released in 1970, and an intriguing juxtaposition of the French New Wave and Italian Neo Realism, this film (directed by Jaromil Jireš; a well-respected, but certainly not a populist, filmmaker) actually brought to my mind a much more naturalistic cross between the visual styles of Murnau (*Nosferatu*), Russell (*The Devils*), Fellini (*Satyricon*) and Bergman (*Cries and Whispers*). Unique and interesting, to say the least!

While there are several brainy, high-concept metaphysical themes explored in *Valerie and Her Week of Wonders* - coming of age, suppression of truth, trust, politics, religion, hypocrisy - I, as a dutiful genre fan, shall focus only on the surface aspect of it as a vampire film.

At first, it's not apparent as a horror movie. Perhaps that's why it's virtually unknown in our circles... but it's every bit as good as, if not better, than many cult classics I've happened upon over the years. (*Lemora: A Child's Tale of the Supernatural* comes to mind, as having been overrated.)

Valerie (Jaroslava Schallerová) is a wide-eyed, pubescent, brunet beauty; an innocent good girl living in a big house alone with her grandmother. She plays in the fields, swims, plays her piano, and goes to church. Childhood is idyllic until one night, a thief comes and steals her beautiful earrings. When she gets up to give chase, she encounters a horrific, white-faced ghoul who covers his countenance with a weasel-mask. The next day, her jewelry is miraculously returned to her, but the gem of her innocence is soon to be lost forever.

In a scenario of dreamlike fantasies, Valerie spies on lesbian nymphs bathing beneath a waterfall; she meets a bespectacled young man who too-soon proclaims his love for her; she witnesses the unhappy wedding of a lush young woman to a withered old man; she discovers that the priest she trusted is a lecherous vampire; and that she is not, as she always thought, an orphan.

The film has a visual signature that can be described only as "psychedelic-noir." Cinematographer Jan Curík's camera pays homage to performance, without sacrificing the ecological beauty of the Czech countryside or the Gothic greatness of the city. The fantasy montages are cut together with a dreamlike sensuality that's both beautiful and disturbing.

A luxurious, often suspenseful fable saturated with shades of Sigmund Freud, Lewis Carroll and the Marquis de Sade, the horror comes in the form of actual, traditional fanged vampires who can shape-shift and cause all kinds of deadly mischief. When Valerie is burnt at the stake as a witch - the story is just getting underway!

One of the things that made me connect with *Valerie and Her Week of Wonders*, fanciful as it is, is the undercurrent of family connections and how these relatives morph from devoted to devouring. Not that I've had this happen in my family, but I always find explorations of these relationships fascinating - which begs the question: How much of an adult's character is nature, and how much is nurture? There's no doubt the movie is a combination of horror and metaphor, but sunk between the fire and the fangs is a human heart.

A NIGHTMARE ON ELM STREET
BY
JOSH MCKEVITT

Graphic Designer/Artist
American Horror Story: Cult,
The Nice Guys, Vida, Freakish
JoshMckevitt.com
Instagram: @Danger_Havok

"Whatever you do, don't fall asleep."
- Nancy Thompson

What's my favorite horror movie of all time? The one that shook me to the core? The one that made me question life's fragility and my little number within it? That movie, without a doubt, is *A Nightmare on Elm Street,* directed by the late, great Wes Craven. This is a movie about a child-molesting dream murderer who can get you in the only place where we're all just sheep.

It was the Summer of 1988. I was 8 and my Mom told me that this was an adult movie that I wasn't allowed to watch. So naturally, as all curious young little people do when put to bed at night, I escaped the chamber of my bunkbed to see what all the fuss is about.

I remember stealthily sneaking into the kitchen and sliding under the dinner table to watch what it was that my parents were glued to in the living room.

As I focused on the dirty grit of the VHS rambling across the TV screen, I remember hearing that cackling laugh. Then that oh-so infamous din of the Springwood slasher's finger knives scraping. The first image I witnessed was a long armed man casually walking down a darkened street alley dragging his metal claws against the walls...SKREEEE!

"WHAT!!! Someone has arms like that? They can do that???," I thought. In true horror fashion, I could not pull away. Transfixed. Then I saw that face. Meaty and slippery. Grinning from beyond the television, and raising his bladed finger, he replies to Tina, "This is God." He then proceeds to chase her down the street towards her house.

At this point, my pants were fully loaded. I was well-done. My brain had been cooked. Someone, please pull me out of this nightmare. But just before I could muster the ability to pick myself up to launch back towards my bed, I hung on for a beat too long to witness this sadistic bastard of 1000 maniacs commit one last raping of my supple eyeballs.

As Tina attempts to get to her backdoor, Freddy pops out from behind a tree and shows her a neat trick by slicing off his own fingers with his gloved hand while making these awful eye movements (from his fingers to Tina and to back to his fingers) and holding that greasy-toothed grin like he just told the funniest joke ever and can't wait to see her reaction.

"Nope."

I ran my fastest back to the bed and pulled those sheets down like an impenetrable wall around me. I barely slept. "What the hell was that?!? I will never be able to view life normally." The events of that night would fixate me forever on the genre of horror.

A Nightmare on Elm Street spawned nine movies total, two television seasons, numerous video game contributions and made a bajillion dollars (bajillion - Webster's Dictionary defines this as a lot). The biggest contribution though, has to be the impressions it has had on millions of people (millions - also in Webster's Dictionary and it also means a lot).

As a kid, I was terrified of these films. After watching just that scene, I was totally warped. It looked real. In fact, I couldn't watch these movies at all until the age of 16 (thanks to a babysitter). I ate up horror from everywhere else at the time though, whether it was slasher movies, demonic possession, you name it. But the boogeyman who could get you when you were most vulnerable? That was it. That was my Achilles' heel. In fact, the televised Pennywise played by Tim Curry did this to me the day it premiered on ABC too. It was something about a force that went to places where it couldn't be controlled or contained. Dreams. Sleep. We were all sheep.

A Nightmare on Elm Street possessed the most iconic film murder weapon of all time. The movie had some of the most original and unique kills and gags in a film. To this day, I still believe they are just as terrifying. Tina, our first victim, is mutilated across the ceiling while her "awake" boyfriend screams out in attempts to rescue her. She slinks up and around the room smearing a bloody trail from her initial wound. As the first kill for Freddy in the film, I would say he's batting a thousand.

From the stretching wall above Nancy while she sleeps, to the blood geyser shooting out of Rod's bed, this film gave visual epilepsy that stalked my imagination. You see, I grew up in a small, haunted, farming community called Black River Falls, Wisconsin. During the exact summer I saw this movie, I was told by my babysitter that there is a man who is related to Freddy Krueger and lives in my own hometown. Coincidentally, there actually was a man in my hometown who was burnt all over his body that the locals called "Crispy." (How nice! I know...) The babysitter and her Aqua Net soaked friends spent an entire afternoon convincing me that this was real. I believed them. They told me the whole story of Freddy (as I had only witnessed the alley scene in the film), informing me that he was a child murderer and was seeking revenge on the parents who condemned him to his current state. The only bit of information that my babysitter and her friends had fabricated was the part that this was based on a real person.

Well...technically.

When Wes Craven wrote the film, it was based on a series of articles in the *L.A. Times* he had read. The articles were about these bizarre and mysterious deaths happening to Cambodian refugees in Los Angeles in the early '80s. During a three year period, three male refugees from the group all died in the same strange way. First, they'd have a nightmare, followed by refusing to sleep (due to what they experienced). Once they eventually gave into slumber, they violently awoke screaming, then died. In fact, the details surrounding these stories were placed neatly and tightly into the *Elm Street* script, giving you an artist's interpretation of the nightmare that had feasted upon those three men.

So I guess you could say, three men sacrificed themselves to give birth to one of the most notorious movie monsters of all time. However, the big and mysterious question remains: what exactly did they see in those nightmares? Furthermore, it's high probability that this mystery is the thing that noodled it's way into my psyche, resulting in what I believe is my favorite horror movie of all time.

POLTERGEIST

BY
RYAN LAMBERT

Actor/Writer/Musician
The Monster Squad, Kids Incorporated,
Short Ends, elephone, Kill Moi
Instagram/Twitter: @RyanLambert111

"This house….is cleeeean!"
Or is it?

In 1981, my parents moved the family about forty-five minutes outside of Los Angeles (where I had grown up) to the small (at the time) community of Simi Valley, California. Needless to say, I was not a happy camper, grumpy as hell, and a total brat. I made some friends, found punk rock, scraped my knees up something fierce trying to skate empty pools, and settled in as a fucked up valley kid.

Sometime in 1982, Chad Anderson and Craig Parker rolled up to a gang of us little fucks and announced a film was shooting not far from our hang spot and we should all hop on our boards and check it out. We wound up outside 4267 Roxbury

Street, where a large crew was filming *Poltergeist*.

Now, I had been "on set" before. I did grow up in LA. They shot *Starsky and Hutch* at Fosters Deli at the corner of the street I grew up on. Travis Schwartz and I used to ride our Huffy bikes down to hang with Huggy Bear and the gang. Yep, we sat in the Gran Torino.

But this seemed different to me. An air of magic floated in and around the block as if something otherworldly had taken up residence. We couldn't get too close and I'm certain we wouldn't have seen too much more if we had, but what I did see changed my mood and the crevasses in my brow. The ghosts in my eyes came to life.

I've heard all the rumors about Toby having trouble directing and Steven having to step in and finish the film. Who cares what's true or not. There are some very Spielbergian shots for sure. When this film was released, my gang was front and center. We were there, man. To be honest, we really had no clue what we were about to watch. I guess I had seen the trailer. Maybe. Possibly an ad in the LA Times Calendar section. Obviously there was no other medium to peep this shit. But I knew. I knew there was something coming. I knew Steven's work, of course. I was crazy for *Jaws*. *Close Encounters* is still my favorite film of all time. *E.T.* pushed me to my actor life. *Raiders* is a masterpiece through and through. But what the hell was this? Where in Hell did this come from? Why are little creepy children singing in a haunted chorus, summoning us all to the closet of doom?

They're Heeeerrreeeeeeee. Ahhhhhh!

I was petrified. I was paralyzed. I was mesmerized. I was hooked.

Why do we scare the fuck out of ourselves? Why do we pleasurize this demonic pastime? (Yes people, I make up words.) It's fun to scare. It's comforting to know you're alive and your blood is pumping. The rush of terror. Embrace the horror. Yay!!

But I'll tell ya. I left the theater in a daze. We all yapped about our favorite scenes. "Dude, that clown!!!" "Holy shit, he ripped his own face off!" "We almost saw Jo Beth's tits as she got thrown around her bedroom by a ghost!"

For me, my favorite sequence comes after the storm of hell-fire. Just when you think it's come to an end. Kaboom. Skeleton Pool. They were not going quietly into the grip of death's eternal crypt. Revenge. "You only moved the headstones!"

Let's backtrack. The best scenario created for horror/sci-fi in the '80s was the struggling suburban family. Let's bring these genres to your own backyard. To set *Poltergeist* in "Tract Home Everyland" made it that much more terrifying.

Mom, dad, brother, sister, older sister. Family. Happy? Nah. Content? I guess. Let's shake up their lives and bring them closer. How do we do that? Ghosts. Mayhem. Take them out of their mundane existence and rattle 'um. What's the extreme? What's the worst thing that can happen to a family? Losing a child. How about you lose a child to another dimension and you can still smell her on your clothes because she passes through you on the back of a demon?

How about you can't run because there is a chance she can be rescued from hell?

Cue Zelda Rubinstein.

Zelda's Tangina is unique in the sense that I'm not sure I had ever felt this close and yet kept my emotional distance from a character since maybe Daffy Duck. Are we on her side? Do we love her or are we frightened of her knowledge and commitment to the cause? Is she the answer the Freeling's have been looking for?

"You said don't go into the light! DIANE!!!"

This family is us in the same way that Jamie Lee Curtis' Laurie was your babysitter. Steve Freeling was my dad. Carol Anne was my little brother. I even kept his closet door open hoping he'd get sucked into another dimension.

Poltergeist isn't my favorite horror film because it's the scariest shit I've ever seen. It's my favorite because it's the first time I understood what a complete, well crafted and executed horror film could be. I usually root for Freddy, Jason or any ol' ghost or shit-can demon. I wanted the Freelings to ward off the bad. I wanted them to win. I needed Caroline to return and have zero knowledge of her residency in goopy monster land. I still think of pushing the TV outside my Holiday Inn room when I've just come from fighting off my own demons.

We will never be safe from hauntings, from ghosts, demons or maniacs. We cannot run from the monsters be it in our imaginations, our lives, or in our own heads. We will always be chased and tortured by our own manifestations. The hero is within and we must all face up to our fears head on, weapons in hand. Don't get too close to that TV boys and girls. You never know what lurks on the other side.

And please don't get my started on an old creepy preacher with flowing white hair and a black flat hat (The Ugly Man) standing at the edge of my bed in the middle of the night.

DRAG ME TO HELL

BY
JONATHAN MARTIN

Writer/Director/Producer/Festival Director
FilmQuest, An Evening with My Comatose Mother,
Kiss the Devil in the Dark, Creatures of Whitechapel
Instagram: @JohnnyAstros Twitter: @FilmQuestFest
BohemianIndustries.com FilmQuestFest.com

I didn't want to see *Drag Me to Hell*. I couldn't tell you exactly why I didn't want to see the film, though. Maybe I didn't like the poster? Perhaps, I didn't take a shine to the actors? The trailer was cool enough, I guess. While I dug me some Raimi, *Drag* just wasn't blowing my skirt up.

Yet, there I reluctantly was at a Cinemark in Orem, Utah. It was a couple weeks after its release, in a sparsely populated theater awaiting a film that, unbeknown to me at the time, would become a major catalyst for where I am today.

I'm going to level with you. I haven't always been the biggest horror guy in the world. Many of the essentials I still haven't seen. My favorites growing up were *Poltergeist* and *Gremlins*;

still two major standouts for me, and that list barely expanded over my development to include the *Evil Dead* trilogy, which I watched in a backwards order.

Eventually, I came around.

Drag Me to Hell opens up with a prologue that I find immensely satisfying. An old-school Universal Studios logo pops onto frame, setting the table. Then, the world we'll be living in during the next 100 minutes is quickly established, and it promises us a place where nothing is to be held sacred. This promise is fulfilled within minutes by offing a cursed Mexican kid who stole from a gypsy, by literally dragging him into Hell in a showstopper before the opening credits even roll.

As the story is set up, we get to know Christine Brown. As played by a totally game Alison Lohman, she's a sweet girl with an even sweeter and supportive boyfriend (Justin Long), who is just trying to get a leg up on her banking career. But therein lies the rub. When given the opportunity to do good by an elderly gypsy woman, Mrs. Ganush (Lorna Raver), she chooses not to, in order to look good to her boss.

You see, Christine is also a bit of a brat. A sweet brat, but a brat nonetheless, which, in Raimi's horror-verse, is more than enough of an indictment.

The film is backed by what is perhaps one of the finest horror scores ever composed by Christopher Young. A playfully dark and delicious theme, instantly iconic, with glorious violins and horns plays throughout. Yet, hidden within is a melancholy piano-based theme for our hero/victim (a common archetype in Raimi horror), Christine, that subtly lets you know that Raimi's judgement of her will not be merciful.

The film still stands out as one of the most genuinely fun theater going experiences I've ever had. The ridiculous jump scares, literally made up of leaves, snap zooms, and a "dancing" handkerchief, got me. The laughs, in which there are aplenty, were genuine and earned, proving that comedy and horror are cosmic lovers that are destined to consistently bring out the best in each other.

I can still recall a woman in the audience laughing while at the same time proclaiming aloud, in what I can only imagine was a delighted whimper, "I'm so scared right now!" Several of us chuckled at this in knowing approval. She was in, man, and so were we.

Too often in horror, I feel that a whole film is about one moment, or one mood. If that fails, the film fails. The concept of less is more has its place, but I'm a more *is* more kind of guy. I like big set-pieces. I like showstoppers. And mercy, does *Drag* have some showstoppers. As great and iconic as the *Evil Dead* films are, *Drag Me to Hell* is the culmination of Sam Raimi's horror powers, and not a trick is spared.

The seance scene is rightfully looked back upon, and imitated, by many filmmakers, especially the up-and-comers. Yet, there are so many gems throughout. We have the aforementioned prologue, but then we also have the truly inspired scene within Christine's car wherein Mrs. Ganush tries to take an object of Christine's in order to implement her demonic curse that is a masterclass of not just horror filmmaking, but filmmaking itself.

Yet the showstoppers, like Christine's bloody nose, flow freely. We're spoiled for choice!

There's the scene in which a fly dances across Christine's face as she sleeps, a slow and steady push on her face is the only camera movement we need to set up the scene and get to a disgustingly joyful explosion of maggots and dirt. The "finale" in which Christine must return her curse upon the corpse of a decomposing Mrs. Ganush in a maelstrom of mud and rain. But you tease us, Raimi! Because we're getting one of the greatest "twist" endings in horror history, a twist that has been telegraphed throughout the whole film, as the promise of the film's title comes to fruition, and Christine is dragged into Hell as her sweetly doubting and supportive boyfriend watches on in terror realizing he never should have started that coin collection as a kid.

There's even a throwaway scene, set in a toolshed, that gives us perhaps the greatest fisting shot in the history of cinema.

By the time the ride ends, embalming fluid will be vomited upon our protagonist. Kittens will be murdered, only to be spit back up down the line. Goats will talk. Tongues will lash. Flies will rub their legs together in anticipation for nasal entry, and pretty girls will be called "pork queens." This movie speaks to me.

By the time I walked out of that cinema in 2009, I was a changed man.

A little over a year later, I would make my first horror film, a short titled *An Evening with My Comatose Mother*. Before we filmed, I requested the entire crew to watch *Drag Me to Hell* in preparation, as it contained within it the spirit of the film I was trying to create; a film that would happen to include a seriously haggard old woman spewing black bile upon our hero, an attractive but bratty girl that we couldn't wait to see get her comeuppance.

I will always consider the film a gift to me and I owe a debt to *Drag Me to Hell* and Sam Raimi as the film and filmmaker that would inspire me to become the filmmaker I am today.

Perhaps, however, the gift is really just a gypsy's curse I was given that in the end will see me sent straight down to Hell? One can only hope.

THE EXORCIST
BY
SARAH NICKLIN

Actress/Producer
Nun of That, Exhumed, The Haunting of Alice D
SarahNicklin.com
Instagram: @SarahNicklin Twitter: @Sarah_Nicklin

Growing up in a fairly conservative family on a steady dose of talking animal movies and *Touched By An Angel*, I didn't even know what horror was or that the horror genre even existed…. until Natalie's 11th birthday sleepover party.

Natalie and I weren't best friends, but we were part of the same friend group of around eight girls. We all had classes together in some way or another or were in Girl Scouts together or played on the local soccer team. The majority of the girls were equally as naive and sheltered from the world as I was.

I had never been to Natalie's house before, even though several of the other girls had. Our core group of girls were all there (along with several others I can't remember). Natalie's family had one of those round, aboveground pools in their backyard, which was a big deal. We spent pretty much the entire day in the pool, taking breaks for pizza, birthday cake, and presents.

Natalie also had an older brother. An older brother who wore black and did martial arts and was in high school and had lots of fancy silver knives and blades with things like dragons carved into the handles. And of course, he was walking around shirtless for the entire party and was happy to show off his knife collection for his little sister's curious friends - of which, there weren't many, just the other Sarah, Michelle, Natalie, and me. The majority of the girls thought he was weird and didn't want to see his weapons collection or watch him practicing with nunchucks in the yard.

Natalie thought her older brother was cool and they got along well. Her favorite part about having a cool older brother who's into all of that "weird stuff" was that he also had "weird movies".

After a full day of sun, swimming, and pizza, a few of the girls had to go home and couldn't sleep over, which left around six of us tucked into our sleeping bags on the living room floor. We watched some typical teenage girl movie and played games like "Light As A Feather, Stiff As A Board" and "Truth or Dare". Then, when we were sure that Natalie's parents were asleep upstairs, Natalie brought out the movies her brother let her borrow for tonight: *The Exorcist* and *Halloween*. Natalie warned the girls that these were scary movies and if anyone was scared, they should go to sleep now, or go sleep in the other room.

Since I had been one of the few girls daring enough to look at her brother's weapons, I thought that I was tough enough to stick it out and watch these movies. Plus, it might be a good way to show her brother that I was cool too and get him to notice me the way I had noticed him. I mean, I had already seen *Hocus Pocus* at another sleepover, how much scarier could this be?

After a majority vote, we decided to watch the one with the girl who was about our age first: *The Exorcist*. If we had chosen

Halloween to be first instead, this essay would probably have a different title.

This movie blew my mind. I had never seen or even imagined anything like it. Most of the girls ended up putting a pillow over their head and trying to go to sleep because they were too scared to keep watching. I was scared at a few parts, but I remember thinking that it was more gross than scary. The girl on the TV looked so gross with her chapped lips and cracked skin and throwing up everywhere….and she was touching her vagina! Never, ever, ever in anything I had ever seen on the TV ever, had a girl touched her "privates" in anyway whatsoever, and now here was a girl violently shoving a cross into them and bleeding everywhere!

I had somewhat recently discovered (about 2 years before) that touching this area could cause fun and exhilarating sensations, but I also knew how delicate it was and how easily it could be hurt if you, for example, used too much baby powder (for external use only) too closely to certain areas after taking a bath. This must have hurt the girl so much!!

I was shocked, but curious and enthralled. It gave me a strange queasy feeling in my stomach… and I liked it. Who would dare to put something like this in a movie?! These were parts of the body that were private and that you weren't supposed to talk about, let alone put in a movie with someone stabbing them!

I felt like I was being welcomed into some sort of dark underbelly secret club that was all wrong. Somewhere that's disturbing and a bit gross and dangerous and that everyone (including parts of myself) was telling me I shouldn't be; and yet, I like it. I liked being here in the darkness, in the gross, with the bad stuff, in the place where I wasn't supposed to be. I liked feeling naughty and nasty; feeling like I had a secret from the rest of the world...that I was drawn to something that others were running away from.

That scene was all I could think about for weeks after the sleepover, and all through *Halloween* which we watched next (although the closet scene also left an impression on me). I would have dreams about it (not nightmares). Dreams where I played it over and over and over again in my head. And of course, I couldn't tell my parents about it or talk about it with anyone, even the girls at the party, because they thought it was horrible and something that was bad (and I didn't want to be made fun of).

I can't really say that *The Exorcist* is my favorite horror movie because there are just so many good ones out there that I like for different reasons. But this is the film that had the biggest impact on me and I will never forget my first time watching it. It taught me about the genre, that this world existed, and about myself. That I'm drawn to things that I'm not supposed to like, and that other people think are dark and gross and wrong… and that those things are awesome, and that there is an entire community of people who are drawn to those things too.

DEADLY FRIEND

BY
BLAKE REIGLE

Director/Writer/Producer
One of Us, Beneath The Surface,
His Name Was Jason: 30 Years of Friday the 13th
www.BlakeReigle.com
Twitter: @BlitzKreigle   Instagram: @BlakeReigle

*D*eadly Friend is a blood splattered after-school special whose creation mirrors its bipolar tone, the *Franken-stein* mythology it alludes to, and made a tremendous impact on me the moment it fused with my psyche. This is not an essay about my "favorite horror movie." However, I'm answering the prompt in terms of a horror movie that had a massive impact on me and my work. While there are horror films that I prefer for various reasons, Wes Craven's *Deadly Friend* became ingrained within my DNA at a young age and its mark can be seen throughout my films.

During elementary school, before I convinced a Blockbuster employee to remove the rating restrictions on my family's account, or mastered the tactic of buying a movie ticket for a PG movie in order to sneak into an R-rated one, I was introduced to a bevy of underappreciated horror films on midday basic cable. Many of the early horror films I watched via basic cable happened to be from Wes Craven. These films came on after the weekend morning's cartoons had finished. If I wasn't playing sports, which I was extremely bad at and loathed attending practice for, I would relish in the empty house and ability to watch hours of television because my parents were dealing with my older brother's sports activities or their own work. Once the kids shows finished for the day, an eerie calm came over the house, the Santa Ana winds blew, the birds stopped chirping, and the rites of passage cinema flowed into the family room. I recall the KCOP 13 afternoon film countdown leading into such films as *Christine*, *Swamp Thing*, and *Deadly Friend*. The latter hit my elementary school brain the hardest.

Deadly Friend served as the ultimate transitory horror film for a suburban kid in the late '80s and early '90s. The setting, score cues, wardrobe, art direction, sound design, production design, casting, character archetypes, direction, all had a striking correlation to television programs and movies aimed at kids because Craven originally made the film for a younger audience. Additionally, the suburban environment in *Deadly Friend* resembled my own growing up in Irvine, California, during the '80s and '90s.

Deadly Friend lured me in with its unsuspecting conventions, then it shocked me with its sporadic scenes of intensity and gore. The tonally bipolar scenes of violence were profound for me because, in many ways, they resembled the world I experienced and was told to fear repeatedly by my parents. Suburbia is designed to appear as if everything is organized and carefree; however, you're still susceptible to human evil and vicious accidents. I found myself in the ER often as a kid; so much so that my nickname became "stitch." Each time, the accidents occurred like a random lightning strike or at the negligence of someone around me. A serene holiday party in a quaint home became a bloodbath after a relative tripped me and my head cracked open on the corner of a table. A water fight on a hot day with hoses and water balloons made the neighborhood kids scream and pass out after I slipped, fell, and deeply filleted my side open on a piece of garage door hardware. A New Year's Eve party ends at the ER after I sliced my finger off cutting an apple. My house was near a four-way stop. At night, we'd often have the soundscape of our peaceful street suddenly shredded by the screeching of car tires, shattering of glass, and crumpling of metal as kids driving too fast had crashed. We'd run outside to see the destruction and then wrestle with the human weakness and mortality before us. Accidents, violence, and gore strike fast in suburbia and quickly create a dichotomy with the environment. Additionally, just like in *Deadly Friend*, monsters live within people. They live inside the people that live on your street, maybe even your own home, and they can sporadically cut into the suburban serenity. I was raised by parents who deeply cared for my well being; so much so they told me stories about how every object and situation could end up scarring or killing me. The way in which the suburban neighborhood can lead to violence in *Deadly Friend* delivered what my parents had prepped me for by displaying a relatable world coupled with the unique genre conventions I was developing a love for. *Deadly Friend* was the cinematic hybrid of suburbia, after-school special, genre storytelling, morality tale, and spikes of violence that intersected in my world at a transitory and important time in my life, just like the intersection of flesh and technology that birthed the BB/Sam hybrid.

Deadly Friend is packed with powerful imagery I fell hard for as a kid. The film foretells its bipolar nature from the title card with "friend" using a childish blue font, and an '80s slasher font used in red for "deadly" — instantly intrigued! BB The Robot's design and voice are absurdly cartoonish. But, it's the stark contrast between BB's design and actions that fired my brain's synapses so hard as a kid. I've always had an overly active brain that constantly views the world in "what if" situations (again, this stems from my parents always pointing out how everything could kill me). What if that cartoonish robot just went nuts and almost squeezed that dude's penis to mush? Whoa! It just did! What if that robot bent that man's hand backwards like snapping balsa wood? NO WAY! It did! A robot defender against awful people in life — definite dream for many kids.

Samantha, played by Kristy Swanson (in her first lead film role), slays on screen. She's the ultimate girl next door. The trailer and television spot imagery with her at the window is one of cinema's greatest images. I love that she goes from cute, red-cheeked, simply dressed girl to pale, blue raccoon-eyed, undead, revenge driven, robot-hybrid bombshell. Her simple look draws you in and endears her to you. After she dies, she becomes a taboo and sexy antihero. Her subtle, undead appearance drew me in further instead of repulsing me. Her appearance following her death is a metaphor for the loss of innocence via destructive means and her vengefulness is a twisted justice against a corrupted world. The basketball kill is one of my all time favorite gore/revenge scenes; the first time I saw it, it exploded my brain, and Anne Ramsey's, simultaneously.

I've always been captivated by human mortality and the *Frankenstein* mythology. Most youth find death fascinating because they struggle with the aging process and not being invincible. I, like many others, pushed against the idea that death could be anything other than an unfathomable length of slow decay. In our teens, we push up against nature's laws to test the waters and see what the limits are (this was true for me as a skater). In *Deadly Friend*, Paul, a scientific prodigy, embodies Dr. Frankenstein in his pursuit to beat death and nature; he decides to play God. Paul, while a genius, can't fathom that someone so young could just be taken and man has no way of fixing the problem. Interestingly, it's man's fallen nature that caused the death in the first place via Sam's alcoholic and abusive father. Paul is emotionally swept up in the loss of innocence and decides against his better nature to perpetuate wrongdoing in order to beat (fix) nature. Paul's prideful decision, like Dr. Frankenstein's, comes with a significant cost to himself, the one he was trying to help, and the world — the evil is perpetuated. In dark moments, we have a tendency to play God, and pridefully feel we can control or beat nature; the *Frankenstein* myth is more about the humbling of us by nature, God, and the cosmos, rather than our control of it. I have an OCD personality; I need order to deal with the chaos of life. At the time I first saw *Deadly Friend*, I kept a vacuum outside my bedroom door to bring order back to the carpet after anyone stepped inside. For an OCD suburban kid like me, *Deadly Friend* was gospel; I knew I needed to calm my OCD tendencies because they could manifest into something that would consume me, like BB reaching out to choke the oxygen from my lungs. While the classic *Frankenstein* movies from James Whale are included on my list of all time favorite films, the ability of Wes Craven, Bruce Joel Rubin, and Diana Hentsell to spin the story in a reflective package for modern youth in the '80s made the mythology come to life even more for me.

Beyond just *Frankenstein* connections, *Deadly Friend* also contained allusions to several seminal films in my upbringing. Once my mom found out I was glued to watching daytime cable horror movies, she took me to the city library and video rental store to check out some genre fare she felt would serve me well. I began watching heavy doses of Hitchcock on VHS and would discover the connections between *Deadly Friend* and *Psycho* (a film I considered writing this essay about). Keeping with its bipolar nature, *Deadly Friend*'s composer, Charles Bernstein, combined two scoring styles for the film. One was modern, performed on synthesizers, and another was classical in style, performed with string instruments, that harkened to Bernard Herrmann's score from *Psycho*. The Herrmann-style score bolsters a particular visual allusion to *Psycho* when Sam is pushed down the staircase to her death by her father. Additionally, the dying close up of Sam on the ground reminded me of Janet Leigh's face following the shower death at the hands of

Norman Bates. Body horror elements (often the result of scientific advancements) via early Cronenberg films such as *Videodrome*, *The Fly*, *The Brood*, and stories of femme fatales (à la Brian De Palma films such as *Carrie*) were also visually present within *Deadly Friend*.

After the mid '90s, I didn't see *Deadly Friend* again until over a decade later. However, it had deeply rooted itself in my brain and erupted later into my work. I didn't realize how much of an impact it had until I watched again in the late 2000s, after making my first feature, *Beneath The Surface*. Both films involved suburban teens losing their love interest (the girl next door) and using academic related tools to bring them back to life. In *Beneath The Surface*, Kahlah is killed by a high school classmate, Shane, who's keen on having sex with her, so he attempts to subdue her with narcotics that he kisses into her mouth. She overdoses, dies, and is buried. Our male protagonist, Ethan, brings her back to life using his anthropologist neighbors witch doctor serum, turning her into a zombie.

Both *Deadly Friend* and *Beneath The Surface* contain similar visual, theme, and plot related elements:

-suburban environments with characters that turn out to be monsters on the inside,

-theme of abrupt death versus natural decay,

-shock of innocence torn asunder,

-catatonic, pale, undead beings that have to be hidden within their forlorn love interest's homes. Sam is hidden in the attic, Kahlah under Ethan's bed,

-Paul has a humorous sidekick, Tom, that's more confident and assertive. This flips once Paul loses Samantha; Paul becomes more assertive and Tom pushes back. The same exists in *Beneath The Surface*. Ethan's friend, Eric, is a correlative for Tom,

-scenes of teaching the undead love interest to move and learn about their world,

-front doors opening for Sam and Kahlah, revealing them from the protagonist's perspective for dates,

-concerned mothers dealing with odd behavior from their sons,

-protagonists studying under the tutelage of renowned college academics which aids in the reanimation of the girls,

-undead girls who get revenge on their violent aggressors,

-undead girls using what hurt them against their aggressors: Kahlah kissing a razor blade into Shane's mouth. Samantha pushing her dad down the stairs,

-inability to control the undead and realizing that death should be respected,

-realizing the painful and destructive gravity of trying to play God,

-shots of an undead girl staring out of a window like a prisoner,

-Kahlah and Samantha run through their neighborhoods, causing havoc, while Ethan and Samantha struggle to find them and right their wrongs,

-Kahlah and Samantha both realize they are abominations and struggle with their existence,

-Paul and Ethan both deal with the moral weight of their actions in tampering with nature,

-final scenes: two men exit a morgue and walk down a hall after finishing with Samantha's corpse. Paul sneaks in and watches as Samantha chokes him with her hands, tears through her flesh, and reveals she's now an evil mutated robot. The final shot is outside the door to the morgue as we hear BB attacking Paul. In *Beneath The Surface*, two men walk down a hall after placing Shane into a padded cell. Kahlah is in the cell and kills Shane. The final shot is outside the cell door as we hear the carnage.

I did not intentionally allude to *Deadly Friend* in my work. It wasn't until after production of the film that I realized the connections. Some critics say a director remakes the same work over and over, i.e., Spielberg's constant return to WWII stories and characters with father issues. For me, I've had a consistent use of beautiful antiheroines that were wronged and then return for vengeance through supernatural, uncanny, or technological means. *Beneath The Surface* involves an innocent girl next-door being killed by a male suitor; she returns from the dead as a zombie and kills him. I made a short, *Touched*, about a man stalked and killed by a female mannequin he fondles. *One of Us*, released in 2017, is a thriller I directed about female reporter who infiltrates a mountain cult of pretty young women that are being manipulated by their male leader. The reporter is abused and — spoiler alert — takes bloody revenge against the cult leader in order to survive and save the other females. I wrote a feature with Dylan Mulick, *Frankengirl*, about an unhinged scientist who builds the "perfect girl" from an assortment of limbs harvested from college students. The deadly beauty ends up at a frat party, killing men that aggressively come on to her. *Deadly Friend* kick-started my brain when I was younger to hone in on stories about women scorned, lost love, and reanimation based morality tales.

Meddling with reanimation and the composite of varying parts can lead to fascinating consequences. While Wes and the producers of the film were at complete odds making *Deadly Friend*, I'm thrilled by the serendipitous outcome. For instance, the producers demanded the inclusion of more gore filled scenes in order to capitalize on Wes' horror stardom and audience expectations. For example, the final scene in which BB/Samantha tears her face off to reveal the evil robot mutation underneath: while the final scene makes little sense, it wrecked my brain as a child…in a good way, to a degree that I wanted to play with similar themes and imagery as a filmmaker. Later on, the final scene takes on new meaning in today's hyper, tech-infused world. It's a metaphorical warning (similar to the *Frankenstein* myths) about the catastrophic consequences of melding ourselves too close with technology.

Heavily underappreciated among critics and audiences, *Deadly Friend* impacted me as a child towards making films of a similar nature, which led to my tenure with Wes Craven's colleague and former partner, Sean Cunningham (*Friday the*

13th). My first feature film led me to Sean's manager, who passed it onto him, and in turn, Sean hired me as an assistant, and later creative executive at Crystal Lake Entertainment. I got to work with Wes on the remake of *Last House on the Left* and tell him how much *Deadly Friend* meant to me growing up. It probably didn't cross his mind during the well-documented trials of making the film, that one day, it would so positively affect and inspire someone's life. It's fascinating to think how watching a movie as a kid on cable TV lead me to direct a film inspired by it and then work with the director.

While today, older audiences might watch *Deadly Friend* with a chuckle or confusion, the true test is to show it to kids on the precipice of their teenage years. I'm sure it will have a profound impact. *Deadly Friend* spoke deeply to me during my childhood and I value its life.

BB! BB! BB!

BEACHES

BY
BILL SHAFER

Art Gallery Owner & Curator/Writer/Actor
Hyaena Gallery, Cohasset Snuff Film,
Serial Killer Culture TV
Facebook/Instagram: @HyaenaGallery

*T*he Exorcist, Demons, Stuart Gordon's *The Pit and the Pendulum*, Carpenter's *The Thing*, *Last House on the Left*, *Dark Night of the Scarecrow*, *Bloodbath at the House of Death*…few movies can match the sheer onscreen horror of 1988's *Beaches*. Directed by Garry Marshall, who haunted my youth with impossible '50s nostalgia, sets the bar high with this melodrama in disguise and I return to it often as a form of self-torture. It's the kind of film cruel parents use to punish and terrify their children; something a shitty girlfriend will make you sit through with the promise of sex that never comes. With every viewing it chews off a piece of your soul, leaving you shaken, fragile, and too tragically aware of your own awful humanity.

It all starts with Bette Midler, a Frankenstein mash-up of cabaret performer, Adolf Hitler, and swamp creature. When her abhorrent maw gapes open, an acidic drool falls like KY Jelly, and she begins spewing the vocal sewage she passes for song. A sane person retches internally. Here, her music takes the form of an incubus and it pushes each note, sans lubrication, into your clenched anal cavity. This is the Beast's power, and it will stay inside you forever like the semen of a thousand pedophile priests. The woman is a harpy. I would easily include her within the pantheon of nightmare creatures the caliber of Pumpkinhead or the gargoyle from *Tales from the Darkside: The Movie*...only Bette Midler is real.

There are flashbacks to ease the tension and space out the jump scares. Child actress Mayim Bialik does an admirable job of lulling you into a false sense of safety, assisted by clever script nods to *Mommie Dearest*. Each scene, however, reminds you that she grows up to be Bette Midler. There is no true solace because of this, and you start to eye the youthful Bialik as a bitchy little Damien Thorn. I'm confident that girl was tainted by the Divine Miss M and has carried the shame of that portrayal with her to this day. The poor thing probably gets PTSD whenever she sees Red Vines.

Barbara Hershey should be the uplifting component of this film, but no. Not only did she used to bang David Carradine, but she also changed her name to Barbara Seagull after accidently killing a bird on set (not in this film, though I assume Bette Midler sprayed her with chicken blood in a Santeria ritual during table readings). Here, however, she's like Erin Brockovich meets Jamie Lee Curtis, trying to fend off Midler's Michael Myers. Bette's putrescent visage remains the focus and mires the film in dread.

Bette pretty much plays herself in this movie, as she rises from filth into celebrity filth. She's jealous of her friend's beauty and pretends she's in Alice, Sweet Alice for a while. Midler happily whores around, abandoning friends and family. Finally, hearing that her once close friend, Hershey, is dying and in need of a heart transplant, Bette pretends she's human and runs to be with her. Unfortunately, Bette Midler has no heart and instead sings a voodoo curse upon us all, entitled Wind Beneath My Wings. The only reason this song has yet to be used in a maxi-pad commercial must have something to do with it being inherently evil. The song serves its purpose as Bette kills her best friend, steals her child, and sets up a sequel, *Beaches 2: Bette Midler's a Cunt*, starring Barbara Eden (which I had always hoped Tom Holland would write, but alas...).

In the end, I'm often shocked at how little acknowledgement Beaches receives from the Horror community. There's a line between fantasy and reality which rarely gets crossed, and it is genuinely unsettling when a film can take you to that point. Hitchcock tried with *Psycho*, but never pushed Perkins to his breaking point. Tobe Hooper came close with *The Texas Chain Saw Massacre*, as well. The problem with these, and so many other examples, is that we always understood we were watching a film. These characters never have a chance of entering our world, but with *Beaches* it is so different. The truth is terrifying: Bette Midler is actually alive and has assimilated, lizard-like, into our society. Bette Midler is a Demon.

DAWN OF THE DEAD
BY
ERIC SPUDIC

Actor/Screenwriter/Filmmaker
Aquanoids, Creepies, Dead Clowns, Dino Wolf,
Killers by Nature, Savage Harvest 2
Facebook: @SpudicsMovieEmpire
EricSpudic.net SpudicsMovieEmpire.com

It was the summer of '93 that I first rented George Romero's classic, *Dawn of the Dead*. A dusty clamshell release from the '80s, from Thorn EMI Home Video. Our family had just gotten our first VCR the year before and I was on the hunt for anything with zombies, machine guns, and explosions.

I was tracking down every war film and horror film I could. It was the living dead, in particular, that really interested me. My first two purchases, I believe, were *Children Shouldn't Play with Dead Things* and *Night of the Living Dead* (the original). I told my parents that we should hit up Suncoast at the mall to find more zombie films.

The next two I picked up were *Zombie* and *Day of the Dead*.

These two really ramped it up from my previous two purchases. Gore galore! Arterial spraying, elaborate effects, spooky atmosphere, and even *gasp* foul language!

It was on the VHS box of *Day of the Dead* that I realized it was the third entry in Romero's "Dead Trilogy". I'm a completist, as are most film collectors, and just had to get that second entry. This was in the days before the internet, and when you had to scour mail-order catalogs to find anything obscure. Even some common titles could be a difficult find back then!

There was a video store in Staunton, Illinois that had a pretty decent horror section. Lo and behold, there was that chewed up, dusty copy of *Dawn of the Dead* on the shelves. I told my dad that we needed to rent it desperately.

We watched it that night and couldn't believe how wild and over the top it was. The family tried to eat dinner as that thing played. Imagine the scene where the biker gets his intestines ripped out. The exploding head! Eugene tearing into his wife's neck!

I became quite fascinated with the effects of all these films. The tape was due back the next day, so I figured I'd watch it the next morning for another watch. The very long two hour plus running time didn't even bother me. Romero really knew how to cut a picture together. It flows, baby, it flows.

My second viewing really let me pay attention to the music, the editing, the characters, everything. I've always been enamored with malls and thought that four people holed up in one is a unique idea. One time, in 2003, my friends and I were heading to New Jersey and made a pit stop at the Monroeville Mall itself in Pennsylvania! It had changed quite a bit, but the escalator and a few stores were still present.

I needed to add this film to my collection, so I found a two-tape set from Anchor Bay in the mid '90s. I had read there were nearly half a dozen versions of this film and was quite happy to see this one was an extended cut. Hell, I even have the HBO cut!

Flash forward to 2018 and I've probably seen *Dawn* a good

60 times at this point. I was really sad when Romero passed away last year. I highly recommend that you see the documentary, *Documentary of the Dead*, which was shot on the set of *Dawn*.

The picture was shot in the cold winter of 1977-1978 for the low sum of half a million dollars. The money is all on the screen for sure. A cast of dozens, numerous zombie extras, a motorcycle gang, a helicopter, tons of weapons, loads of blood, and more.

The making of the film is just as interesting as the film itself. Italian horror maestro Dario Argento was a big fan of *Night of the Living Dead* and approached Romero about producing a sequel. So George flew over to Italy and banged out the script in less than a month. The two later teamed up for *Two Evil Eyes*.

When I have the money someday, I plan on having a *Dawn of the Dead* tribute room. I have already owned a few shirts, posters and the novelization. There's a board game out there too. Snatch it up.

One of the highlights of my life was having Ken Foree come to one of my birthday parties. He's still pretty active in the business. Gaylen Ross went on to appear in Romero's *Creepshow*. Scott Reininger was teaching acting at one point and even made a cameo in the remake. "Flyboy" David Emge starred in the Michigan-lensed *Hellmaster*.

This film will never bore me. It's comedy, it's horror, it's a western, it's a drama. Everything is here. You can tell the cast and crew had a blast working on this one. Bring me more zombies!

FRIGHT NIGHT
BY
B. HARRISON SMITH
Director/Writer/Producer
Death House, Camp Dread, The Fields, 6 Degrees of Hell,
Zombie Killers: Elephant's Graveyard, Garlic & Gunpowder
Class85.com
Twitter: @HarrisonSmith85

Of all the horror movies to pick, and with the original *Jaws* being the movie that made me want to make movies, I am selecting Tom Holland's 1985 vampire hit, *Fright Night,* as my favorite. Like the film itself, that's a sleeper hit answer. No one would suspect it.

And it has nothing to do with horror.

I suspect *Jaws* will be a likely choice by many writers. It's my favorite movie of all time, regardless of genre. I don't know if I qualify *Jaws* as horror. For me, it's an adventure film; a drama on the high seas and no different than *Moby Dick* in that regard. I saw the film in a theater when I was eight years old in 1975, and I left that theater knowing I wanted to make movies for a living.

So, why *Fright Night?* The memories attached are powerful, and while many see it as a valentine to old school horror, I saw it as a swan song. The film's theme touched me, and even watching it in a theater at 17 years of age, I got what Tom Holland was trying to say.

Fright Night is about mourning. It is about time passing us by. It is a sad reminder that perhaps our better days are behind us. When I watch it now, I feel maudlin when done. Not only do I miss the summer of '85, I miss my childhood that was perfectly tapped by Holland's film. I grew up watching those old horror show hosts like Peter Vincent. I was terrified as a child by Hammer's Christopher Lee *Dracula* films, and as I grew up, I watched monsters like Frankenstein's Monster, Dracula, The Mummy, and The Wolfman, get replaced by Jason Vorhees, Freddy Krueger, and a multitude of psycho slashers.

Roddy McDowall's Peter Vincent (A play on Peter Cushing and Vincent Price), admonishes William Ragsdale's Charley Brewster that his generation doesn't appreciate the creatures that preceded the '80s run of slasher films.

"Apparently your generation doesn't want to see vampire killers or vampires either! All they want are demented madmen running around in ski-masks hacking up young virgins!"

I was a virgin when I saw *Fright Night,* and by the end of that summer, I was not. The film helped bond me to the girl I would surrender it to. We were both "old souls" perhaps? However, she was the hottest girl I'd ever dated in my young life, and I was head over heels. I was an assistant manager at the local mall multiplex and had the privilege to watch all the movies after hours any time I wanted. I threaded up the film in our smallest house (It was an end of summer, dog days release. No one expected it to be a hit) and we went downstairs to a 200 seat theater to watch our own private viewing.

Instead of making out, we were glued to the screen. At two

in the morning, I went upstairs, re-threaded the machine, and we watched it again. In hindsight, how did I ever get laid?

I identified with Charley Brewster, an average suburban horror fanboy with a girlfriend he wanted a tad bit more than the monsters on the local cable show called Fright Night. He wanted to believe in vampires and monsters, and one night… he gets his chance.

His idol, Peter Vincent, is a washed up B-movie actor who longs for days gone by. That summer of '85, I identified. I graduated that June and was a rock star class president who had adventures worthy of *Risky Business* and *Fast Times at Ridgemont High*. Now, it was over. College was on the horizon and it was all new…and scary. I was in love with this beautiful girl who was as witty and smart as she was easy on the eyes.

I was naïve and young. What did I know? However the film, which was fun, appealed to the old soul inside me. I felt badly for Peter Vincent. I identified with Charley. The good old days were gone and the future was scary for them.

Even Chris Sarandon's vampire, Jerry Dandridge, is a lost soul. Gone were the days of terrifying whole villages and holding mortals in terror. The love of his life was gone and he was forced to live with a daywalking roommate in modern suburbia. The vampire's best defense is that no one believes in it. But what fun is that?

Even though Jerry risks exposure in declaring war on next door neighbor Charley, it's likely the first time he felt truly alive in a couple of centuries. Jerry was back in action and we suspect that the bland name of "Jerry" wasn't his real one. He's been forced to hide out to survive in some of vampire witness protection program. His eternal life is boring and likely to stay that way as his victims become more sophisticated and less superstitious over the decades. Charley and Peter are the first real challenge in a while and he seems to enjoy it.

Fright Night gave fuel to the sentimental pilot light I had kept on for horror. It made me miss being a boy on the eve of becoming a man. Ironically, it would resurrect the vampire film and pave the way for *Buffy the Vampire Slayer* and unfortunately, *Twilight*. It was a reminder to me that horror wasn't as fun as it used to be, and in many ways, had lost its innocence somewhere along the line. Just like I was about to.

I mean, yeah, vampire movies are about sex and seduction. That's their core. We know that your chances of getting some action is to take your significant other to a horror film. The adrenalin flows, the blood races, and there is the hanging on part that gives us the touching, tactile aspect of the genre that others do not afford.

The *Friday the 13th* and even *Halloween* films gave us (and at that point, continued to offer us) cynical portrayals of teens and sex. Have sex and die. *Fright Night* served a reminder that sex was passion, and sometimes that love and passion hurt like a stake driven through our hearts. Not long after viewing the film, I had sex with this girl. I proposed (during a fifth late night screening of *Fright Night*) at 17 years of age and thought this would be my life...with this girl...forever. We would be in mad, passionate love forever. I would save her, like Charley saved Amy, from anything nefarious.

As most of you know, that just doesn't happen. We broke up by that fall. I went on to Penn State, and from there, I went on to Los Angeles to work at Universal...all by 18 years of age.

Tom Holland's film serves as a reminder to never forget the old days and what inspired us. While we can mourn and miss what once was, time does indeed move on. All of the characters at the end of the film are different than how they started.

I wanted to make a movie like that one day. While I was already making films and had my own cable comedy TV show at 16, *Fright Night* served as a touchstone that I would never lose. Holland had a similar theme in his script for *Psycho II* which would also serve as a major influence on my directing debut with *Camp Dread*. Holland's themes of "time gone by, sentiment and nostalgia" hit home with me and *Fright Night* brought it all into focus.

My grandparents are gone now. Dr. Shock, Uncle Ted,

Zacherley, Vampira…they're gone too. Yeah, we have Svengoolie, but he's a male Elvira. Now, we have *Mystery Science Theater,* and oddly, that gives me far more appreciation and sentiment for the old B-fodder than the modern hosts aping the old ones.

The girl I was going to marry is now in New York City and with someone else. We stay in touch here and there through the magic of email—a few lines to let each other know we are still alive.

However…almost every email of those two or three a year hellos invoke a line from *Fright Night.* It's our touchstone and maybe, it keeps the pilot light on to guide us back to each other every now and then. Even if it is only to just say "hi."

We just lost George Romero, a man who gave us more than he got back from fans and the industry. He was Peter Vincent in some ways, making good old horror with passion, only to see it aped by a weekly TV show that was built entirely off the sweat and infrastructure he created. If only that show's fan base knew it and cared to know it.

So, thank you, Tom Holland. Thank you for more memories than you could have ever thought a film like *Fright Night* could provide. Thanks for reminding us of some pretty great days gone by, and allowing me to see it as it was unfolding around me.

Thanks for making films that inspired me to be a filmmaker, and now, a pretty successful one. "You're so cool, Brewster."

ABBOTT AND COSTELLO MEET FRANKENSTEIN
BY
ROLFE KANEFSKY

Writer/Director
There's Nothing Out There, The Hazing,
Nightmare Man, The Black Room, Party Bus To Hell
RolfeKanefsky.com
Facebook: @Rolfe.Kanefsky

W ell, it's safe to say that when my father introduced me to the films of Abbott and Costello at the age of four, they changed my life. I fell in love with comedy, making people laugh, and cinema. Growing up in New York, I watched their films religiously every Sunday morning at 11:30am for roughly the next twelve years. Of their 36 features, the one that made the biggest impression and is still considered by many to be the best horror/comedy ever made is their 1948 classic, *Abbott and Costello Meet Frankenstein*. The title is funny in of itself since Frankenstein is probably the only one they don't meet in the movie. They meet Frankenstein's Monster, Dracula, the Wolfman, and in a creative cameo at the end, even The Invisible Man.

I was around six years old when I finally saw the whole movie because I could never make it past the first Lon Chaney Jr. werewolf transformation. It scared the hell out of me and I ran from the room. But then one day, I braved it, lasted another ten seconds, and heard Costello tell the Wolfman to "Get his dog off the phone," and I started laughing. It was the perfect blend of serious horror followed by a big joke. It made fun of what was happening on the screen, but didn't stop the terror either. This is why this movie is so great. The monsters play it straight and the whole storyline could have been a legitimate Universal horror movie. The plot of Dracula trying to find the brain of a simple man so he could control Frankenstein's monster is a real premise that could have worked with any leading man of the time. But putting the most successful comedy team in the world in the lead allowed the story to work as both a comedy and a horror movie. Many years later, I met one of the screenwriters, Robert Lees, at a screening of the film and got his autograph which I still treasure today. I also own the script.

The blend of comedy and horror became the basis for my first professional feature film, *There's Nothing Out There*. Abbott and Costello was a huge influence, and to this day, there is still a very strong sense of fun to most of my horror movies. People don't always get my sense of humor since I'm not working with world famous comedians, but it is strongly present. Their blending of witty banter, puns, and physical comedy have never grown old for me. I still laugh. And Universal's famous monsters still are effective in the movie as well. Last time I saw this movie in a theater, the audience still roared, and how can one not when Lon Chaney confides in Costello, "...in a half an hour, the moon will rise and I'll turn into a wolf" to which Costello replies, "You and twenty million other guys."

But surprisingly, Abbott and Costello do very few of their famous routines in the movie. There is no "Who's On First?"

or "Do you have two tens for a five?" sketches. In fact, Costello was very worried that the film would bomb. He didn't find the script funny. The story goes, he didn't even like the film until his mother saw it and told him that it was probably the best work he's ever done. From that point on, he loved it. And audiences loved seeing them fight the monsters. Hence, came *Abbott and Costello Meet The Invisible Man, Abbott and Costello Meet Dr. Jekyll and Mr. Hyde,* and *Abbott and Costello Meet The Mummy* in the following years. All horror/comedies that worked then and still play today.

The horror/comedy genre is a tricky one. Many try and fail. It's a delicate, thin line to balance. As a filmmaker, I love the challenge, because when it works, watching an audience react with screams and laughter is no better feeling. It's entertainment of the highest order. And any fans of *Fright Night, An American Werewolf In London, Night Of The Creeps, Tremors, Re-Animator, Evil Dead 2,* and *Shaun Of The Dead,* should check out the film that helped inspired the makers of those films and create a genre that will never go away. There is no denying that *Abbott and Costello* is classic cinema and a shining example of how to properly combine the genres beautifully.

If you're a filmmaker trying to make a horror/comedy and you get responses like "It's too funny to be scary and too scary to be funny", remind the "powers-that-be" that Abbott and Costello made it work, kept Universal alive back in the '40s, and could have even owned the studio because of their success. So, stick to your guns and remember as one of the taglines that *Abbott and Costello Meet Frankenstein* states: "They'll scare you 'til you laugh for more!"

JOHN CARPENTER'S THE THING

BY
ERNIE TRINIDAD

Journalist, Screenwriter, Actor
www.ErnieTrinidad.com
Twitter: @ErnieTrinidad
Facebook: @ErnieTrinidadFilmMaven

W hen you're just a kid, seeing a movie at the theatre required planning, and in my case, would often require a guardian of at least seventeen years old. In the late 1970s and early 1980s, horror films weren't exactly on the top of the "must see in the theatre" list. Prior to 1982, a year many consider the greatest genre year in cinematic history, there really weren't that many horror films released, and I only watched a few of them theatrically. It was less about what I wanted to see, but what my father was willing to take us to or even allow us to see. My dad didn't mind taking the kids to scary movies, but I didn't go that often. In 1980 I saw *The Fog* and *Saturn 3*. In 1981 I saw *Halloween II*. Genre standouts like *The Shining, Friday the 13th, Friday the 13th Part*

2, Prom Night, Ghost Story, The Final Conflict, The Howling, and *Wolfen,* I didn't see until they were shown on cable. John Landis' *An American Werewolf In London* was the very first VHS movie we ever rented. It was at a video store found inside the Cinnaminson Mall in Cinnaminson, NJ, and I think it was close to six dollars to rent. This brings us to 1982. I think 1982 is the year that my love for the movies really took shape. In 1983, I actually started keeping a log of what I've seen theatrically (unfortunately, I've lost that log). I recall watching a fair amount of the genre films released in 1982 on cable, but I do remember seeing a vast majority of the horror films on the big screen. *Amityville II: The Possession, Halloween III: Season of the Witch, Friday the 13th Part III* in 3D, and *Poltergeist,* were all theatrical experiences. However, that year, there were two horror films of note, because I actually went to see them twice.

At the time, science fiction and action adventure films were my favorite genres, so I would typically see my favorites a few times. But for me to see a horror movie more than once was a rarity. One of those films was the great George A. Romero and Stephen King collaboration, *Creepshow.* It was such a fun film. The other film really affected me in some surprising ways. It was a film which my eleven-year-old self from South Jersey thought was cool, but it wasn't until much later that I found it to be the masterpiece it is regarded to be today. It was a film where, as a kid, I had to quietly say "Yeah, fuck you, too," whilst describing one of my favorite scenes. Most significantly, it was a film where my younger self, who was often squeamish during gory scenes, simply could not take his eyes off the screen because he was amazed by what he was seeing. It was June 1982. My dad took me to see a new horror/science fiction film at the Budco Millside Twin in Delran, NJ. The film was directed by John Carpenter and starred Kurt Russell. The film was *John Carpenter's The Thing.*

I knew of both Carpenter and Russell and was a huge fan thanks to the previous year's *Escape From New York.* At the time, I considered *Escape* to be Carpenter's best film, because

I was an action fan and I thought that it kicked some serious ass. In the old days, movie trailers were only shown in movie theatres, so I likely first heard of *The Thing* in the pages of *Fangoria*, *Starlog* or *Famous Monsters* magazines. Just looking at the on-set photos and the stills from the film, I was likely grossed out, but knew I had to see it. I do recall feeling squeamish while looking at a photo from *Friday The 13th Part III*. It was a still of the aftermath of Jason cutting the hand-walker in half. The blood and guts were in glorious color. The blood was crimson red, and the intestines were glistening. Around 1980 or 1981, while visiting Los Angeles, I bought an issue of *Famous Monsters* at the Farmer's Market in Hollywood and was grossed out by the black and white photos from *Friday The 13th*. I remember feeling grossed out by a moment in *Galaxy of Terror* where a shard penetrates Sid Haig's arm and we see it moving up the arm while underneath the skin; or seeing part of Harvey Keitel's face hanging off Hector's head in *Saturn 3*. Watching these moments as an adult, I was rather amused that they weren't as visceral as I remember them being, but could certainly see how it may be rather unsettling for a young kid. I enjoyed being scared, but I certainly didn't always have the stomach for the gore. Ultimately, my father thought I could handle it, otherwise he wouldn't be taking me to see these films. Thanks, Dad!

This new sci-fi/horror movie was a remake of Howard Hawks' production of *The Thing From Another World*, which I'm sure I've seen on *Dr. Shock* on a Saturday afternoon. Both films were based on John W. Campbell Jr.'s *Who Goes There?* I'm not even sure I've ever read it, but seem to recall seeing it reprinted in *Twilight Zone Magazine* or another zine of its ilk. When I was younger, I was more about the pictures and not the words. You've heard the joke about reading *Playboy* for the articles. Well, I would buy the genre magazines for the pictures. I remember having a magazine confiscated in grade school. It was *Prevue Magazine*, and while I had it for the movie news, the teacher took it because of the scantily clad, buxom babes found within (but that's another story). Going into the film, the pictures I've seen are all I knew about it. Even with the fore-knowledge that there was going to be some gruesome imagery in the film, I don't think anything prepared me for how I would react to what Rob Bottin and his effects team put on display. From the moment MacCready and the men of U.S. National Science Institute Station 4 first laid eyes on The Thing, the film featured vast amounts of sinew, blood, slime and gore, and I simply could not pull my eyes away. I was absolutely riveted. This eleven-year-old boy from the suburbs who would get a bit squeamish during the gory scenes was fully absorbed into the bloody magic transpiring on screen and didn't feel ill at all.

Looking back, I would have to say I was caught up in won-dering just how they did it. The makeup effects were done prac-tically, with a smattering of stop-motion work. At the time, I don't think I've ever seen anything like it, nor on such a grand scale. The dog transformation scene. The autopsy scene. The Norris defibrillator and transformation scene. The blood test sequence. By all accounts, I should have been running up the aisle, trying not to hurl my Milk Duds, but I couldn't get enough of it. This was undoubtedly the reason why I wanted to go back and watch it again. I'd seen my fair share of creature features prior to this, but I don't think I watched one on such a human scale whose creatures were so convincing. Mind you, I grew up in the seventies and eighties, so my early diet of mon-ster movies was comprised of *Godzilla*, *King Kong*, giant insects or any other horror fare you may see on TV on a rainy Saturday afternoon. I suppose Ridley Scott's *Alien* may have served as an appetizer to Carpenter's main course. Even then, I remember being grossed out by the chest-burster scene. Funnily enough, I forgot my glasses when we went to see *Alien, so* my brother and I shared his. I was wearing his glasses during that scene. I think he planned it that way.

I think *John Carpenter's The Thing* really opened my eyes to the makeup effects and visual effects world, and I actual-ly found a disconnect which allowed me to truly appreciate the artist's work, not just in horror films like this, but films in general. This rendered me susceptible to the horror genre as a whole, so when video stores really began cropping up every-where, my palate expanded exponentially as I took in films that I likely would not have if I was still feeling a bit queasy from the gore. *The Wizard of Gore. Make Them Die Slowly. Zombie. The Beyond.* I found myself watching films from directors I'd never heard of before like Fulci, Argento, Lewis and Cohen. Surprisingly, I once got into trouble for bringing home Tobe Hooper's legendary *The Texas Chain Saw Massacre.* I watched it, but Mom was not happy about it. This revelation was very much like when, at the age of fourteen, I fell in love with west-erns. At the time, I never bothered to watch one because they looked rather dull to me. Seriously, what's so exciting about riding horses and bar room brawls? Give me the big guns and martial arts! Then I saw Lawrence Kasdan's *Silverado* and soon enough, I was watching westerns from Ford, Eastwood, Le-one and Hawks. Speaking of 1985...that year featured some of the bloodiest and goriest horror films ever made. I don't think I'd have caught them in the theatre if Carpenter's film hadn't already strengthened my resolve. *Day of the Dead*, *Demons*, *Re-Animator* and *The Return of the Living Dead* were game changers in terms of make up effects and are amongst my all-time favorite horror films to boot.

In 1982, my eleven-year-old self found *John Carpenter's The Thing* to be a really cool science fiction/horror movie. I loved it for the visual and makeup effects, but that's about it. Present day, thanks in part to my understanding of story and character in terms of filmmaking, I consider it to be Carpen-ter's best film, and one of my all-time favorite science fiction/horror films. The film not only opened my eyes to the creativity and the tools used to make a film, but I now knew the names of the artists just as well as those of the stars and directors of such films. Tom Savini, Dick Smith, Rob Bottin, Greg Nicote-ro, Robert Kurtzman, Howard Berger, Stan Winston and Rick Baker are pioneers who helped shape and continue to transform the craft. Most importantly, *The Thing* got me over the hump to be able to stomach the goriest and most vile films that filmmakers can imagine. As a horror film fan, that resolve is definitely something worth having. It was John Carpenter's exceptional film that helped me find it.

      P.S. - I realize I failed to mention how Carpenter's film is a grand exercise in suspense, acting, writing, editing, directing, composing, cinematography. For these reasons and more, I believe *John Carpenter's The Thing* is his best film and one of the best science fiction/horror films ever made. Now, if you disagree, I must say with the utmost respect "Yeah, fuck you, too!"

SLEEPAWAY CAMP 2: UNHAPPY CAMPERS

Actor/Director/Producer
2 Jennifer, Serena Waits, Irrational Fear,
Ugly Sweater Party, #From Jennifer
LAHorror.com
Twitter/Instagram/Facebook: @LAHorrorCom

Horror is such an odd genre. My favorite horror films tend to be dark, bleak, and perverse. There's just something about raw human emotion; pain that one person can inflict on another; endings that leave you not relieved, but mortified. Movies that sit in your gut and make you rot inside. I adore the vile, depraved visions from filmmakers that dare to dream something out of the worst realities that humans experience. But then again, in a genre that blankets films like *Cannibal Holocaust* and *Henry: Portrait of a Serial Killer*, it also covers films that are much lighter, sillier and most of all, campier than others. My top 2-10 would include only stone-cold, chilling horror; but my number one spot (or my desert island movie, if you will) is a quirky '80s slasher film called *Sleepaway Camp 2: Unhappy Campers.*

When I was growing up, I bought horror movies at a rapid pace. I'm sure most film lovers go through these spurts time and again, but between the ages of 14-17, I was probably averaging about 10 DVDs or tapes a week. I would go to every used movie store, video store, book store, whatever - and buy all of their clearance horror titles regardless of how crappy the movies looked. That said, not all of the films were my favorite, but every now and again you'd find something worthwhile. And then, on very rare, rare occasions, you'd find a diamond in the rough. A film that would change your whole life. A film about a group of happy campers.

I had never heard of the *Sleepaway Camp* series when I stumbled upon the DVDs at a used book store. Parts *1, 2,* and *3.* Now, while movies were cheap, I decided that I'd only buy *Part 1,* you know, to see how it is and decide if the sequels would even be worth a shot. So I go home and plug in *Sleepaway Camp,* with absolutely no idea what it was about or with any expectations. If you're a fan of horror, I'm sure you can guess what happened next. I was absolutely riveted. Floored. I adored the film, and the ending left my jaw on the floor. *Sleepaway Camp* completely caught me by surprise, so the following morning I went back to the bookstore to buy *Parts 2 & 3.*

Now it's tough to make a horror sequel that lives up to the original, and maybe after being blown away the night before, I wasn't expecting *Unhappy Campers* to be as good. But that said, when I watched the film, I had a serious emotional connection to it. It was bizarre. But if you're a film enthusiast, I'm sure you know what I'm talking about - when you watch a movie and it hits you hard. That's what happened to me, and to be honest, I'm not entirely sure why.

The thing that pulled me most into *Sleepaway Camp 2: Unhappy Campers,* was the sincere and criminally underrated performance from the film's lead, Pamela Springsteen, who portrays the all-grown-up psycho killer, Angela Baker. I have seen a ton of horror films, but I truly believe that this is one of the most genuine and chilling performances in horror history. The character of Angela is so complex and full of genuine emotion, it reads in every scene she's in. Couple that with some truly great supporting characters, some really disturbing kills, and of course the bummer: nobody that I adore survives the ending; and I had my new favorite film of all time. While most write it off as campy and cheesy...I truly think it is one of the most heartbreaking, genuine horror films ever made.

Now that said, this is an '80s slasher movie that is not let's say...the best...except it is. The quality itself is lacking at moments, and of course there are some highly ridiculous scenes. But unlike other campy slasher flicks that popped up around the same time, I truly BELIEVE that the world created in *Sleepaway Camp 2* exists. I truly felt the pain of these campers and the frustration that Angela feels as she tries to fit in. As absolutely bonkers as this sounds, I wanted to be at that camp with those campers in that movie. It just seemed like the perfect place, and I was sad that I wasn't a part of it. I was literally heartbroken when the film ended, but the first thing I did when it was over was look at the box for *Part 3* and check if Pamela Springsteen is in that as well. To my absolute joy and relief, she was. I turned it on immediately.

Part 3 was absolutely fantastic as well, but I'll admit it did not have the same impact as it's predecessor. That said, after I watched the films, they were all I could think about. I did a little sleuthing and saw that Pamela Springsteen hadn't done much acting work after the films, which totally shocked me because I was about to watch her entire catalogue. So I used my Google skills and found she's an active photographer that has done some pretty sick stuff. I decided I had to reach out to her.

At this point of my life, I was about 17 years old, living in a Wisconsin suburb, but of course I had dreamed of one day going out to Hollywood to make horror movies. I mean, isn't that everyone's dream? But that said, at the time, it was still a distant idea, not a tangible reality. It was the awkward phase in life when you know you are going to have to start doing something...start making some big decisions...but you hold the fear of making the wrong one...going to the wrong college...choosing the wrong major...which causes your life to tailspin. But sometimes, the universe sends you a sign you just can't ignore.

My e-mail to Pam Springsteen was polite. I simply complimented her performances, told her (in the least creepy way possible) that they had an impact on me, and asked for advice for someone who wants to act and make horror films for a living. I did not expect a reply, but low and behold, a few days later, one came in. Angela Baker, from *Sleepaway Camp 2: Unhappy Campers*, the most important film I had seen in my entire life, e-mailed me back. And it was amazing, so kind, and thoughtful. Not just a sentence or two, but a solid page of feedback and words of inspiration, as well as insight to her own personal experiences working on the series. Here is one sentence that stood out to me, that I still try to live by now over 10 years later:

"Keep studying, keep writing, expose yourself in as many ways and as much as possible to the real world of filmmaking... if it feels right and you're passionate about it, you're on the right track, and you can do it."

This was and continues to be the coal in my internal furnace. Now, years later, I make an active effort to be as productive as possible. To work on as many horror projects as I can. To shoot my own films if nobody is casting me in theirs. To do people favors and build a network of collaborators I can trust. I've still got a long way to go, but I truly owe a lot of where I am today to that little film.

Inspiration can come from a lot of strange places, and I never would have guessed that my light bulb moment would come from a trashy '80s slasher sequel that most people (unfairly) dump on. But it did, and I've never looked back. In fact, my one and only tattoo reads "Oh, I'm a happy camper!" This is a way to remind me to stay positive, stay focused and that someday, I might be able to make a film as excellent as *Sleepaway Camp 2: Unhappy Campers.* Now, sing it with me:

Oh, I'm a happy camper!
I love the summer sun!
I love the trees and forests!
I'm always having fun!

Oh, I'm a happy camper!
I love the clear blue sky!
And with the grace of God, I'll camp until I die...

JAWS
BY
ESTHER GOODSTEIN
Producer/Writer/Actor
The Black Room, Nightmare Man,
Spreading Darkness, Sex and the USA, One in the Gun
Facebook/Twitter/Instagram: @CasualEsther

Truth is, I don't think I would be making horror movies if I hadn't been hired as script supervisor on a fun little horror/comedy with writer/director Rolfe Kanefsky. I am an actor first, with a BFA from UArts, and a lifelong writer. I fell into script supervising to help a friend with her project and discovered an immediate love for it. I've forever been a gal who wants to know everything and that's the scripty's job. Fun!

I produced Rolfe's next flick, *Jacqueline Hyde*, and I was hooked. I considered choosing this as my subject, but it felt a little like shameless self-promotion, so perhaps another time.

Instead, I chose *Jaws*, the only film to make me consider a different vocation and to alter my behavior for life. Pretty powerful stuff, right?

I saw *Jaws* with my father when I was just shy of 9 years old. Yeah, my dad was freaking awesome. Most of my friends were not allowed to see it, so I got to tell the story of *Jaws* about a dozen times. A few lied to their parents, and we all went the next weekend. It was the first time I saw a movie twice in the theater and I loved it even more the second time. A couple of friends got mad because it was so scary, but that's what I loved about it. They got over it by the time we graduated high school.

Back in elementary school that fall, our teacher asked us what we want to be when we grow up. I surprised myself by answering, "I want to be an actress or a writer...or a marine biologist." This brought confusion to the faces of my friends who had never heard me say anything like that before. The lunch table talk was crazy that day. I had always loved the ocean. I loved Earth science. And yes, I was inspired by *Jaws*. They were incredulous, but accepting, as good friends should be.

Over the next couple of years, I said it often. My parents were supportive – truly supportive of everything I ever wanted to do or try. They got me a microscope and other science kits. I liked seeing what my eye could not. Same reason I love photography. Seeing a new perspective. I still love that. I continued my dance, voice and acting classes throughout. Also, my mother is a superb singer and actor, and has a degree in microbiology. So in my family, it's all good.

In junior high, I had a great science teacher who encouraged my passion for discovery. We had chemistry for the first time, which I loved like any future mad scientist would, and I dissected a frog with the best of them. Mine had eggs. So cool. Then, we had a talk one day after school and he explained which courses I should take to prepare for the life of a scientist. There was a lot of math. I was out. Immediately I realized I didn't want to be a marine biologist, I wanted to be Richard Dreyfuss in *Jaws*. Well, the girl version.

My foray into science is but a blip compared to the permanent change in my own behavior.

FLASHBACK

A three-year-old Esther is propped up on Daddy's shoulder as he wades us into the Atlantic Ocean. Over his broad shoulder, I can see the Atlantic City Boardwalk, my mother, and brother Ben on the sand. We went out past the breakers and were bobbing with the tide. It was the best place on earth. "Further, Daddy!" I cried again and again. My father was a tall man and an Army lifeguard. He was cool with "Further, Daddy," and we went out far.

I kept looking up and down the shore to see if there was anyone further out. If there was, I would say it again. "Further Daddy". I needed to be furthest out. It was imperative that it was me and the ocean. The ocean was a spiritual force to me. Very personal. Very deep.

FLASH-FORWARD

The first time I went to the beach after seeing my beloved *Jaws*, I had no idea, no warning, that such a profound change had taken place.

I started in as I usually did, walking straight into the surf until I could swim, then diving under the breakers. I was nine by now and Daddy no longer carried me into the water. I was alone. Just me and my beloved. Coming up past the breakwater, my usual deep breath would not come. I had no breath. Couldn't catch it. Everything felt different. Cold. I wasn't sure what was happening to me, but it felt like my skin got tight.

I was frantic. Looking up and down the shore, I was definitely the furthest out, and it filled me with dread. I realized I was watching the swells in front of me, searching for fins, and that my old friend the ocean was scaring the crap out of my little mind. I turned and swam back a bit until I could see others out beyond me.

I could breathe again. Felt the bobbing and rocking of the

gentle waves moving my body; finally relaxed.

I still love my old friend, the ocean. I still visit when I can, and I have never lived far from a coast. I can visit the middle, but I need to live on an edge. Where the sand meets the sea. It's still where I find peace. But I always look up and down the shore…to make certain that I am NOT, "Further Daddy."

Never Again.

Damn You Spielberg.

HALLOWEEN
BY
MATT MERCER

Actor/Filmmaker
Contracted, Contracted: Phase II, The Mind's Eye,
Beyond the Gates, Madison County, You or a Loved One
Twitter/Instagram: @MercerShark

In July of 1986, ABC aired *Jaws* as the Sunday Night Movie. I was six years old, visiting my grandparents in Culpeper, VA, and, with my mom's "okay", they let me stay up late to watch it to the end. It changed my life.

For the next few months, I literally *couldn't stop thinking about it.*

I convinced my mom to buy the VHS cassette of *Jaws* and I watched it constantly. Watched it until certain sections of the tape (mainly the attack sequences which I replayed over and over) were so demagnetized that one couldn't make out what was happening on-screen entirely. Adjusting the tracking on the VCR didn't make a lick of difference. Just as Bryan Adams played his guitar until his fingers bled…I played *Jaws* until the tape was in shreds.

I became a shark fanatic. I wanted to be Matt Hooper, the Richard Dreyfuss character. I projected a future in which I became a marine biologist - specifically an ichthyologist - who studied all kinds of sharks. I'd get myriad scars from my encounters with them. I'd live the Hooper Life, traveling the world to find giant sharks and study them. Amity Island, Brisbane, aboard the Orca or the Aurora... bring it on. I'd read every book about sharks. I was ready.

I tried to convince my mom we needed to switch our summer beach trips from Myrtle Beach, SC to Amity Island. It'd be safe... they didn't have a shark problem anymore. The issue I encountered was when I looked on a map to find Amity Island, I could only find an Amityville in New York. The heck?! Where was the island? Must be some mistake.

We had a fish tank and I cruelly tried to tie a soda can to one of my pets with a string to see if I could recreate the yellow barrel scenes from the film. It didn't work. Beta fish are slippery. And fast. (As Hooper would say, "Fast fish.") I also "recreated" several attacks from *Jaws* in the bathtub with little green plastic army men and a rubber Great White. These reenactments came to a halt when my stepmom couldn't find her McCormick red food coloring and I got in trouble for stowing it under the sink in the bathroom, having used almost all of it for the attacks.

When the school year started, my first grade teacher Mrs. Jones expressed concern when, for the first show-and-tell of the year, I didn't share my shell collection from a summer trip to the beach, or cookies I'd baked with Mom, or a woodshop project made with Dad... No. No, no, no. I performed Quint's death from *Jaws* in all its glory. I laid on the floor in front of the entire class, and while kicking and screaming, slid down the stern of the Orca into the shark's mouth. In my mind, it played beautifully. I flailed wildly. I kicked at the imaginary chomping maw of the shark. I maneuvered my body to make the slide seem natural, as if the floor were at an angle. I aped

Robert Shaw's giant blood- puke. And, I very clearly recall the army of blank stares I got in return from my classmates when I was done.

Further explanation of the scene and the events leading up to it didn't help, and Mrs. Jones quickly invited me to sit down before the details became more grotesque. Enough already. I wanted to yell at them, "Don't you get it?! I've experienced this incredible thing, and so help me God, you're going to take the journey with me!"

What had this movie done to six-year-old me? Why couldn't I stop thinking about it and wanting to relive and recreate its thrills over and over in any way possible? Was any of the movie real? How did they make it? Was Robert Shaw really killed by that shark? What was the path to more of these thrills?

These questions started to be answered that Christmas, when my grandmother (who had become aware it was *Jaws* 24/7 for me, and was also super-cool apparently) gifted me a copy of *The Jaws Log*, a firsthand account of the making of the movie *Jaws* by one of its screenwriters, Carl Gottlieb. Now, this book was a bit advanced for someone my age, and although I was a fairly advanced reader, I didn't entirely get it. My film-making lexicon was limited at that age, obviously. But it made one thing clear for me: the movie wasn't "real" and a group of people had indeed made it. They'd put it together, piece by piece, over a relatively large chunk of time, photographed it, and the process was all spearheaded by one person, a director, Steven Spielberg. *Jaws* wasn't some crazy event that happened to get recorded by some folks near the beach. It was manufactured, piece-by-piece, and came out as this scary movie. Great.

So, that means there must be more of these movies. Right?

Not long after finishing *The Jaws Log* (probably early '87 by now), I asked my mother one morning while getting ready for school, "Mom, what is the scariest movie you've ever seen?"

She thought for a moment. "Hmmm. Probably *Halloween*."

Halloween? There's a horror movie called *Halloween*?! My kid-brain caught fire. My mind started to conjure what the movie might be, and the dream-reel didn't stop...images of demons in the autumn dark, monsters snatching trick-or-treaters off the street and dragging them into the woods, creatures with glowing jack o' lanterns for heads...what the hell could this film be? She wouldn't tell me. And thus began a massive campaign on my part to see the movie. I wouldn't let up.

I mean, I really begged, and begged, and begged my mother to rent it. I could handle the movie, but I couldn't handle waiting until I was older to see it. Her answer was a flat "no," until honestly, I don't recall how her change of heart exactly happened, but after a few weeks, she finally relented and agreed to let me see it on one condition: she had to watch it first, and I had to turn away during anything involving nudity or sex.

Deal.

Next thing I knew we were headed to Rent-A-Tainment, our local video store in Newport News, VA. It had a bright yellow sign shaped like a strip of unspooled celluloid, the store's name in big bold letters on top of that - a beautiful beacon at dusk. I remember that night vividly. Prior to the video store, we'd grabbed some dessert, something called frozen yogurt (a fresh concept in the mid-'80s, and "healthy" alternative to ice cream!) from a new place called Yogurt's Inn. (Newport News small business owners in the mid-1980s were super clever in the store-naming department.) Walking into Rent-A-Tainment, I went straight to the Horror section, blowing past all the sections (Disney, Family, etc) that had been safe, easy, and allowed in the past...

And there it was. The VHS display box of the Media Home Entertainment release of John Carpenter's *Halloween*. The iconographic box art with the jack-o-lantern and a big hand with insane vascularity, swooping down with a gleaming butcher knife in its grip where the last ridge of the pumpkin should be... it stared me in the face. Glorious. It held so much promise.

We raced home and popped it in...I don't recall if my mother ended up doing a pre-screening or not (I think she just winged it from her memory), but I do remember the experience of watching it that night. From the opening credits, as the camera slowly pushed into the glowing, flickering pumpkin, I was completely entranced. I couldn't move. And it just kept getting more and more intense, every element of the film perfectly calibrated to scare the living hell out of me...out of the audience. It was one of those rare times the movie lives up to the quality you've been cultivating in your head...even though it was nothing like the movie that had been playing in my head prior to seeing it.

But watching *Halloween* was more than just a defying of expectations.

That night was the peak viewing experience of my (short) life up to that point. Part of that experience was I'm sure due to the fact that I was a young, impressionable kid watching a truly scary movie for the first time, but I don't know that another film has worked on me like that since. At least not in that way. It was everything all at once. Every element of the film wrapped around me like a dark blanket of dread and terror that, as the film played on, tightened around my mind and body until I was suffocating. But I couldn't look away. I just wanted more. Where *Jaws* had imbued me with a sense of wonder and thrills, *Halloween* was scarier and more pure...it was perfect, shadowy atmosphere and visceral terror honed from the simplest (but well-crafted) elements. *Jaws* was my gateway into horror and showed the possibilities of film, but *Halloween* was the real deal and blew my world apart. I think I watched that two-day rental copy ten times that first weekend I saw it. To this day, I watch *Halloween* at least three times a year. I'm still obsessed. It still takes me on an incredible journey and inspires me to no end.

So much has been written about *Halloween*...the making of it, its success as a low-budget independent film, how it ushered in and created an entirely new "slasher" subgenre and era of horror films, and the techniques that made it so effective. I won't regurgitate that here in great detail. If you've seen the movie, and read about it, you know these things already. The techniques Carpenter uses are transcendent and game changing. The music. The mask. Dean Cundey's cinematography. The way he fills the 'Scope frame. It's a flawless intersection of technique, storytelling, atmosphere, and scares. There's an unrepeatable and unmistakable alchemy that makes the film what it is. In other words, it's all about how this story is told, not necessarily what it's about. The style these elements create, added to the simplicity of the film, is the formula that makes it so effective.

In a small Midwestern town, Michael, a six-year-old boy murders his sister on Halloween. Fifteen years later, on Halloween, he escapes the sanitarium where he's being held, and goes back to his hometown to kill again. That's pretty much it.

Simple.

Over the years since the first time I saw the film and the countless times since, I've often thought about what the key factor is (beyond the aforementioned style) that makes it my favorite horror movie. I think the answer lies somewhere in its restraint. In a way, it's not what Carpenter did do, it's what he didn't do that makes *Halloween* special. The film is nearly bloodless. He uses the frame to create a visual language that puts us on edge, as opposed to throwing gore at us (not that there's anything wrong with that…I love a good bloodbath, but I'm glad it's not here). Carpenter also suggests, but doesn't overexplain, the subtle supernatural aspects of Myers. Mystery begets better terror. The first of these touches is the fact that it takes place on Halloween. In its development, the film was originally called *The Babysitter Murders* (which sounds scary already), until one of the producers of the film, Irwin Yablans, suggested it take place on (and be called) Halloween. This idea was a stroke of genius, because although Carpenter (wisely) doesn't use the dark holiday to explain Michael's killing spree, the fact that Michael "activates" on All Hallows' Eve adds a layer of bizarre uneasiness to his motivations. It comes from somewhere dark and inexplicable. Carpenter knew better than to have a ritual or séance or possession aspect to explain the killer's actions...it's just simply the date when Michael goes home to kill. And that's enough.

Another subtle touch: the methods used to make Michael the personification of Evil. As Doctor Loomis says in the movie, Myers "isn't a man." Well, he looks like a person, and he's shaped like a human, but measured doses of strange behavior suggest there's something more going on there...something more at the wheel inside Michael than just himself. He doesn't talk, he only breathes. He wears a mask to kill. Later, he wears coveralls taken from a tow truck driver that he's murdered, his "costume". He inspects his kills in a curious way; after murdering one kid, he tilts his head back and forth. Later on, he sets up a haunted house of corpses as a gauntlet of terror for the main character, Laurie. He also doesn't seem daunted by injury. When Laurie stabs him, he doesn't stop. It's these touches of character that make The Shape scarier. Where is this weirdness coming from? These traits culminate in the climax, where Michael is shot six times and falls from a balcony...and then disappears.

Thus, by the end of the film, these supernatural hints (and the Myers character) have fully developed and transformed into theme, the idea being that evil never dies. It can't be killed. It will always be there, looming in the dark, ready to strike without warning.

Halloween started me on a constant diet of horror movies, and there are many in my "favorites pantheon". *Alien* transported me aboard a ship in deep space and showed me creatures I couldn't have seen in my wildest dreams. *Psycho* catapulted me into the mind of an isolated killer living a double life. *Jaws* had already whisked me away on an adventure on the ocean and given a glimpse of what lurked beneath the surface of an unknown world.

But *Halloween* was in my backyard. Every night. Staring up at me from between the clotheslines. It turned the most basic location, the most identifiable place, suburban America, into a terrifying landscape. A place of darkness and danger. Haddonfield didn't feel like South Pasadena, CA, where they shot the film. No, *Halloween* felt like it was happening in a small Illinois town. It felt like my hometown in Virginia. The streets in it felt like my street. The houses felt kinda like my house.

Halloween didn't just take me to another world; it turned my own world into something new. As I started my own career, I took that with me.

DEVIL DOLL
BY
CHUCK PARELLO

Producer/Writer/Director
The Hillside Strangler, Ed Gein,
Henry: Portrait of a Serial Killer 2, Dr. 420
Facebook/Twitter: @ChuckParello

I first became aware of my favorite horror film, *Devil Doll*, right after I was hired to publicize home video releases at MPI Home Video, a film production and distribution company in Oak Forest, Illinois. I was paging through MPI's catalog past advertisements for such tasty fare as the notorious *Faces of Death* series, when suddenly my eyes widened and I could feel my heart pounding in my chest.

Staring up at me from the catalog was some wicked artwork for the film *Devil Doll* - a ventriloquist dummy in a cage with flames all around it - with a tagline that read "Is it flesh or wood, man or monster?" and I instantly knew this was something I needed to see. So I went and found a review copy of *Devil Doll* and planned on watching it that evening.

Full disclosure: I'm a total freak for ventriloquist dummies! I don't know why, but there's something about their googly eyes, hinged jaws and ruby red lips that brightens up my whole demeanor and puts a sick smile on my face. Although I'm not a ventriloquist myself, I'm a proud poppa to 2 sassy ventriloquist puppets (Jerry & Junior) and some of my friends refuse to call me anything but Puppet Boy, a moniker no doubt bestowed on me because of my ventriloquist puppet-like habits of cracking dumb jokes and being occasionally irritating.

So I brought the VHS copy of *Devil Doll* home to the crappy apartment I shared with my brother and a guy who lived in our closet. And after guzzling many brewskies, the three of us sat down to watch it.

The first thing I noticed about the black and white 1964 film, which was shot in London, was that the title was misleading. It should have been called Devil Hypnotist/Ventriloquist, as the most devilish character in the film was not Hugo the Ventriloquist Dummy, but rather his creepy hypnotist/ventriloquist master, The Great Vorelli (Bryant Haliday, Voodoo Blood Death.)

The ultra imperious Vorelli, who wears a cheesy fake beard to hide his identity, is a total asswipe to his dummy Hugo throughout the entire film, to the point where you actually feel kinda sorry for the little wooden guy, locking him in a cage at night, denying him ham and wine, making fun of his sawdust filled stomach, calling him "ugly" and "a common puppet." No wonder a fed up Hugo pulls a knife on Vorelli at one point! But committing damnable puppet abuse pales in comparison to the other dastardly deeds the loathsome Vorelli has up his sleeve, like tricking Hugo, who is obviously played by a little person in some scenes, into murdering his buxom assistant Magda, after she threatens to expose him to the police, and hypnotizing and seducing the voluptuous heiress Marianne Horn, played by scream queen Yvonne Romain (*The Curse of the Werewolf*), so he can take all her family's millions and transfer her soul into a ventriloquist doll, just like he did (SPOILER ALERT) to his old assistant Hugo back in Berlin in 1948!

But Vorelli's wicked plots might just be foiled by Marianne Horn's American reporter beau Mark English, played by William Sylvester (*2001: A Space Odyssey*). English, who has a dimpled chin that looks like it could swallow you whole, becomes fascinated by the hypnotist/ventriloquist and launches an investigation that uncovers his past as a medical doctor who dabbled in mysterious Eastern magic. Or Vorelli might be stopped by something else entirely - not that I'd ever give away the film's shattering climax!

Devil Doll was directed by Canadian Lindsay Shonteff, who made several other low-budget thrillers in London, and the simple, yet also oppressive cinematography is by Gerald Gibbs. Needless to say, the initial inebriated screening I had with my bro and the dude who lived in our closet was a success! We all found the flick to be a complete joy from the first frame to the last, laughing and crying as we cheered Hugo on to his next acts of Vorelli defiance. And then we watched the film over and over again, parroting it's best lines (You cannibal!) like we were *Devil Doll* disciples with an unofficial secret language only we understood and laughed at.

In doing my research for this essay, I discovered *Devil Doll* was featured on an hilarious episode of *Mystery Science Theater 3000*, where two robots and this dude screened the film while cracking jokes about it. Knowing this made me feel happy and vindicated my love for this puppeteer masterpiece, as there are obviously other *Devil Doll* disciples out there!

There have been other films featuring creepy ventriloquist dummy/master relationships (think 1978's *Magic* starring Anthony Hopkins), but only *Devil Doll* packs an emotional wallop that feels like a punch in the guts. So if you're looking for a beyond awesome movie featuring an eerie ventriloquist doll, crack open a brewski and give *Devil Doll* a whirl.

THE RETURN OF THE LIVING DEAD

BY

JACK BENNETT

Writer/Director/Producer
Anthrax: Blood Eagle Wings, Bloodworks, Caprice,
Blood and Guts with Scott Ian,
Fun Sized Horror's Good Night
Never Surrender: A Galaxy Quest Documentary
Twitter: @ThatJackBennett

I had never watched an entire horror movie, beginning to end, until I was eleven years old. By that time, I had read multiple Stephen King books, pored over horrific illustrations by everyone from Stephen Gammell to Bernie Wrightson, but for some reason, I drew the line at scary movies. My overactive imagination might have been giving them too much credit. I assumed that any given flick, adapted from King or otherwise, would be every mental image that had been conjured by those stories now brought to life before my eyes with absolute reality. I always pictured being plunged into a deep well of terror as if movies had the power to spike my mind with *Videodrome* levels of vividness...not that I knew to make that reference yet. A few seconds of the PG-13 rated *Dreamscape*, peeked at from around the corner of the couch on which my older brother and his friends sat watching, was enough to send me running upstairs as if the scene onscreen possessed the ability to give chase. Still, there was something that kept drawing me back, dipping one foot in the water while fearfully eying the deep end. I had been roving a public library and somewhere between periodicals and novels I came across the "Official Movie Magazine" tie-in for *The Dream Child*, facing out from the shelf like a sneering rebuke to the child enrichment surrounding it. I cracked open that book directly to a set-photo of Freddy tearing out a young girl's guts and feeding them to her. That was all my subconscious needed to terrorize me for weeks. Yet, I'd still go back to that same library and sit between aisles, turning the pages of book after book, cataloging long lists of horror films, sometimes with screencaps. At that age, horror movies were like a girl whose photo I would gaze at in a yearbook, but if I saw her on the playground I'd run and hide.

Long before that, when I was seven or eight, I was on summer vacation in Delaware with my family and, as rainy days at the beach invariably convinced us to do, we found ourselves at the movies. I came this close to being snuck into the theater for my first R-rated movie until my brother pointed out the poster art; green-skinned decomposing dead-eyed creatures staring at me from around a tombstone. The text that read "They're back from the grave and ready to party," provided little comfort to a young mind picturing that vision of dread at feature length. Posters and production stills had planted in my fertile young imagination and overgrown like Jordy Verrill's lonely death; there was no way I would sit still for what I was convinced would be a protracted waking nightmare.

So sometime between eight and eleven years old, the following happened: my parents had forbidden my brothers and I from watching television during the week, meaning Saturday morning cartoons were a big event throughout my childhood. I'd wake up before the rest of my family and tromp downstairs. By 11am every morning, the fun was signaled to be over with the flash of an animated web and my favorite show, *Spiderman and Friends* (by 11:30am all there was to watch was golf and I'd excuse myself to more valuable pursuits). I eventually realized that the earlier I got up on Saturday, there seemed to be no shortage of cartoons. I finally got up so early one morning that there were no cartoons at all, but switching to HBO there was *Fraggle Rock* and my routine was set in cement. From then on, I got up every morning at 7am, turned on *Fraggle Rock*, and began my epic Saturday. One morning, I got up so early and *Fraggle Rock* hadn't even started yet, forcing me to watch a dry interstitial called *Braingames* (I still remember the sniffling announcer sadly announcing "*Braingames*…is now…over," as the title erased itself).

Then one Saturday I got up so early that when I switched on the TV and turned it to HBO, the set roared at me "live BRAINS!!!!!" as a young man tried to violently bite through his girlfriend's skull.

I sat transfixed for what I would find out much later was the last twenty minutes of *The Return of the Living Dead*. By the time my bleary-eyed parents shuffled downstairs at 7am, squinting to see what the hell was going on, the only sight that greeted them was their silent, wide-eyed little boy staring at *Fraggle Rock*.

This began a trend as I would naturally wake up between 6 and 6:30 in the morning, and HBO would stop their R-rated programming at seven o'clock. I would turn on the TV and wake up to the climatic scenes of everything from *Re-Animator* to *Fright Night* to *Evil Dead 2* (which I saw the ending of many, many times, often with my younger brother in tow, and referred to as "the groovy movie" until I was in my early teens. In my twenties, a version of that anecdote won me the "Book of the Dead" edition of the Anchor Bay DVD in a contest with Chud. com). The abstract idea of a horror movie had been terrifying but the reality was fascinating, and O'Bannon's film made a bigger impression on me than more sophisticated media ever could. If you're at the age when the possibility of good guys losing doesn't even occur to you, a film that ends with every single surviving character being nuked by the people trusted to rescue them was like someone reaching into my brain through my eyes and reconfiguring the system.

Oddly enough, having seen the end of the movie first, I never really questioned what came before it. An inappropriate twenty minutes viewed under covert circumstances didn't really open me up to sounding boards within my family, so I made no attempt to question why someone would crawl into a lit crematorium, how that slimy gangly zombie got melted in the first place, and just what Freddy and Gina's relationship was like prior to his attempts to eat her brains. What I had seen existed in its own sealed off bubble in my mind, I saw what I saw and that's all I knew about that. One important breakthrough had been made, though; the playground crush was now a fully formed attraction.

Flash-forward to my teens, when no one was pre-approving my movie rental choices anymore, and a quick glance at the back of the VHS case on the video store shelf confirmed that (1) this was the "brains!" movie that someone tried to convince me to see in the theater when I was seven, and (2) this was indeed that movie where everybody gets blown up at the end. Finally watching it resulted in the same excitement a *Breaking Bad* fan gets from dead characters showing up on *Better Call Saul*, or a *Star Wars* fanatic on their first viewing of *Rogue One*. "Oh my god that's the guy who climbs into the big oven! And that's the guy who tries to eat his girlfriend's brain! AND THAT'S HOW THE ZOMBIE MELTED!!!"

I've now seen *The Return of the Living Dead* more than any other horror film and it remains my favorite zombie film for a variety of reasons. It's helped by my general association of horror movies with punk, at least in terms of ethos; like rock n' roll, the genre is fundamentally unpretentious, no matter how much pretension gets heaped on top of it. And like punk, horror is transgressive art, hitting us in the gut and fulfilling the aggressive aspects of our nature (and horror remains as effective whether it's as precise as "Janie Jones" or as sloppy as "Forming"). I have no idea why Dan O'Bannon decided on punks as his young protagonists (or what typical LA punk rockers were supposed to be doing in Kentucky, but I knew punk lifers in Virginia, so the supposed incongruity helps endear the movie to me even more), but it instantly shifts the movie away from typical mid-eighties slashers, in which normality gets represented by clean-cut, commercial-ready teens (the exceptions being Beverly Randolph's lamb-soft ingenue and John Philbin's New Wave goofball, as even chiseled Freddy has the red dye and earring). The choice puts *RotLD* closer to *Suburbia* and *Repo Man*, and while this might be more of my personal baggage showing through, it also positions the film as smarter and slyer than what Roger Ebert used to call the "Dead Teenager movie." Upon introduction, our "victims" are already a little hardened, less innocent than the unwitting prey in your average horror flick. It creates a similar effect to the Space Marines in *Aliens*; when you see a tough character scared shitless, the threat seems that much scarier.

Though nostalgia has colored my appreciation of *RotLD* (I truly doubt the average horror fan would see it for the first time today with a more enthusiastic response than "Oh, okay, that was cool"), it does hold up, thanks to memorable designs, O'Bannon delivering on clever shot choices, and a solid script. Creating an ensemble of distinctive, colorful characters with a dozen different mini-arcs to be set up and paid off, O'Bannon gives every scene juice, either with an indelible character beat or the kind of new mythology twists that genre buffs crave (What if total dismemberment still couldn't deter a zombie's attack? What if zombies were intelligent? When exactly does an infected person lose their personality? What would it feel like to be a zombie?). The movie feels like a series of set pieces, even when the action is as sedate as a medical examination (of two living people with symptoms of rigor mortis). The frequently cited humor doesn't even alleviate tension so much as heighten a growing sense of dread; when a severed arm grabs at Ernie the coroner's pant leg, the audience stifles nervous giggles instead of guffaws of relief. For all the exploitative standards (including Linnea Quigley playing a character who spends most of the movie wearing only a short vest and thigh-high stockings), the movie's titillating concessions don't seem gratuitous so much as bleak; our personal style, relationship peccadilloes and coveted sexuality are of no importance to the creatures clawing their way to eat you alive.

It's all part of the vision of an intelligent, gleeful genre deconstructionist. Dan O'Bannon was hired by John Russo to give a script polish to his *Night of the Living Dead* spin-off before Russo showed great foresight and humility by stepping out of the way of O'Bannon's ideas. Possibly because of the writer-director's passion for them (or just the need to get a film in the can after original director Tobe Hooper dropped out), but just as likely because Russo saw how hip, pervasive and potentially profitable O'Bannons ideas could be. Never self-conscious for more than a second ("You mean the movie lied?!?" is the only line that makes my eyes roll), O'Bannon's confidence in his characters and concepts creates an alternate reality to Romero's, one that cheekily refers to *Night of the Living Dead* as a movie within O'Bannon's universe. The split allows us to share a joke with the filmmaker without inviting comparisons between the films, with zombies as different from each other as the vampires of *Near Dark* are to the ones from Salem's Lot. O'Bannon looked at the job at hand and instead of being content with something familiar and simple, he got ambitious and went for broke.

That certainty of vision and surplus of invention are what's most often missing from modern horror movies, as directors work overtime on atmosphere without servicing a fresh idea. O'Bannon knew the most effective horror movies are effective tales, and every ghastly development of *The Return of the Liv-*

ing Dead is delivered with the relish of a campfire story. For my money, the pre-credit sequence is as close to perfect as horror-comedy has ever gotten, with pages of expository dialogue delivered colorfully under the guise of training the new guy. After settling into their routine, one innocent inquiry from that new guy Freddy (Thom Matthews) to the old hand Frank (James Karen, whose performance throughout the entire movie is somehow simultaneously over-the-top clowning and grave, credible pathos), inspires what is simply a spoken story, not too sensational to be unbelievable, that builds enough tension, it becomes an entire short film unto itself (Karen's grinning read of the line "typical Army fuck up," deserves its own Saturn Award). The first time you see the movie, you have to believe Frank is pulling the kid's leg, up to and maybe even after the big telephone jump scare and the question "wanna' see 'em?" Finally a great punch line; Frank boasts that the sealed drums containing certain death were made by the "U.S. Army Corps of Engineers," gives the steel a good solid pound with his hand, and it promptly busts open. It's an auspicious, surprising introduction, from the sheer amount of dialogue to the reveal of a canned zombie to the "You're going to need a bigger boat," level laugh accompanying our initial nose-dive into grisly horror.

I hesitated using the term horror-comedy in the above paragraph. Horror uniquely encompasses any other genre; some are domestic dramas, others are satire, relentless action, or character studies, and examples of the genre play as fable, as allegory, as sensationalism or as smut. The mercifully short-lived argument that a new trend of "post-horror" or "elevated horror" exists both misses how generously wide the genre's umbrella extends since even the first examples of expressionistic silent cinema, and ignores a near century of classy, high-minded horror films to sit alongside the cheap thrills. While westerns or other period films are defined by their setting, we define horror by where the material takes us; dark places, with death or worse as a promising rather than repellant expectation from the audience. Moments that we'd never want to experience in real life become thrilling as a vicariously experienced fantasy. With that primary distinction, the tone of a horror film can be as wildly divergent as *Dead Alive* is from *The Brood*, as *Let the Right One In* is from *The Texas Chain Saw Massacre*, as *Martyrs* is from *The Haunting*, as *Don't Look Now* is from *Brain Damage*. All bonded in the brotherhood, sharing the disreputable distinction of being horror. I'd personally argue that famously celebrated horror-comedies *An American Werewolf in London* and even *Shaun of the Dead* should be rightfully categorized as horror movies, the comedy in each a distinguishing characteristic that doesn't dilute the sincerity of their genre bonafides. So *Return of the Living Dead*, not a simple comic derivative of Romero, is a genuine horror movie, with genuine humor but even more grimness. Much of it plays like a test scenario to gauge the unlikelihood of humanity surviving a zombie outbreak, however small or contained. Shortly after gaining sympathy for the standoffish protagonist punks by bringing out their vulnerability, the movie is then unrelentingly cruel to them. Feel sympathy for a character? Too bad, they're going to die. No movie that contains the menacing off-screen moans of an undead boy taunting the girlfriend he's desperate to attack, while her companion prepares for their mercy killing, could be classified as "comedy." While I love *Day of the Dead,* even with those endless jingoistic monologues, I feel like anyone actually in this situation would act more like *Return of the Living Dead*'s ensemble. Some of the kids fall apart emotionally before being torn apart literally, some of the characters buckle down and get resourceful, while others let themselves get bossed around, and two characters slowly, painfully, become zombies in a way that emphasizes the personal tragedy of the genre more than Romero's admittedly brilliant movies ever did. The humor in *RotLD* comes out of a familiar sensation; we're so completely screwed all you can do is laugh about it.

Also of note; if you got pissed off by *28 Days Later* ushering in a new dawn of running zombies, look no further for that frustrating concept's inauguration. Of course I agree with the

belief, attributed to Romero, that zombies are as fast or slow
as the decomposition of their muscles dictate. I've gone over
The Return of the Living Dead so many times in a handful of
different versions, and frankly, the movie is so ingrained in me
I can't even begin to debate the idea of running zombies on
any other terms than this; when they bullet out of the shadows and decimate a police blockade like a swarm of locusts, it
is scary. Likewise, the throaty moans of "BRAAAAINS," from
the undead, debuted in this very film and infecting pop culture
for decades to come (a modest but unexpected hit, *RotLD* was
widely seen and respected in genre circles. To the point where
I am convinced that Michael Crichton, knowingly or unknowingly, referenced Tina's repeated squeal of "They left us!" in the
original *Jurassic Park* novel).

Though the cast contains nobody you're likely to know
better than the Dad in *Freddy's Revenge* or the dude who killed
Jason as an adult (though you are reading this book, so it's that
much more likely that Thom Matthews, Clu Gulager, Linnea
Quigley, James Karen and Don Calfa are all household names
to you), my favorite aspect of O'Bannon's film is the vivid characters introduced casually, no one dominating as the lead and
therefore nobody guaranteed survival by their position on the
call sheet. Taking inspiration from Howard Hawks, O'Bannon
gives his ensemble energetic dialogue and distinguishes each
character with costume design and well-defined personalities.
Even when a line reading occasionally falls flat or feels like amateur hour, I still feel grateful to O'Bannon for creating distinctive people at all (and taking time to rehearse the actors
like they were, y'know, actors, rather than just attractive canon
fodder). Threats to our humanity, be it individual or collective,
are still the bedrock of horror, and no matter how cynical the
movie treats life, it reminds us that horror doesn't work if life
is without value. I'm always surprised to find I get more moved
by a brief goodbye between two scared-but-tough middle-aged
men in the last act of *The Return of the Living Dead* than any
scene in any Oscar-bait movie (the "Bert, that favor that you

owe me," moment, in which Don Calfa's empathetic eyes and the quick disappearance of Clu Gulager's winning smile say it all). Doubly so for James Karen's exit, conceived by the actor, a poignant and chilling moment scored by a maniacal Roky Erickson song that taunts Frank's ultimate sacrifice (the MGM DVD needlessly "fixes" the soundtrack to drop out the music and focus on Karen's tortured scream, O'Bannon's apparent preference, though the excellent Shout! Factory Blu-ray restores the original, far more effective theatrical mix). Speaking of the music, the soundtrack is packed with TSOL, The Damned, The Cramps, and other '80s mainstays who seamlessly fit into the smirking sci-fi menace of Francis Haines and Matt Clifford's score (different releases contain different combinations of songs, but none of the changes compromise the movie's effectiveness). Rather than eerie tones or a straight-faced horror pulse, the songs and score again contribute a dark twist to the film; the music is not on the side of the heroes. When an otherwise silly skeleton rises from the ground and pops open its intact eyes, 45 Grave screams "DO YOU WANNA PARTY?!?" celebrating the impending evisceration of our human characters as party time.

Dan O'Bannon's only other film as director, the Lovecraft adaptation *The Resurrected*, is not terribly compelling despite good performances, though the occasionally screened workprint restores his sense of story and timing to the point of being much more engaging than the film that was released. *The Return of the Living Dead* remains his scruffy masterpiece, a nastily grinning curb-stomp to the day's rinse-repeat formula of horror sequels/spinoffs. The film reveals not just O'Bannon's bleak sense of humor ("Send more paramedics!") but also his borderline subversive strain of human empathy; Jewel Shepard's bitchy banter stops dead at a request to be held, Linnea Quigley's confrontational sexuality instantly transforms into vulnerability once a burning chemical rains down on her skin, and by the time the threat level is absolute, the punks have lost any pretense of defying authority just as the straights don't give a second thought towards trying to save their lives (a misguided switchblade threat from Scuz is punished a few scenes later, but by bad luck rather than retribution). There's something immediate and almost idealistic about how everyone's differences go out the window in the face of a common enemy. In O'Bannon's world, no group gets singled out when it's the living versus the dead, at a certain point we're all just trying to survive. O'Bannon's widow Diane shared another clue to Dan's humanism; the zombies bite through skulls with their teeth, a frightening image that is impossible to imitate successfully in real life. Despite O'Bannon's rounded character and frequently described crankiness and eccentricities, the idea that he couldn't risk even that unlikely of a real-life copycat crime on his conscience suggests a fundamental decency. A literate fan of classic sci-fi and literary horror who grew up dreaming of telling his own stories, O'Bannon was a great hand at matching convincing characters to an inventive genre trope (with so many genre films missing either one or the other that made him a treasure). I'm glad he was around and got his work out there, with this one film he almost singlehandedly got me into horror movies. For that I owe him a great deal of thanks.

BRAIN DAMAGE

BY
JAMES CULLEN BRESSACK

Bethany, Pernicious, Hate Crime,
If Looks Could Kill, To Jennifer
Instagram/Twitter: @JamesCullenB

Henenlotter is a genius. There's no denying that. When it comes to off the wall, kooky characters, he's got them in spades. When it comes to imaginative creatures with personalities, nobody does it better. When it comes to just pure zany, weird and out-there concepts, no one really has the mind that this guy has. If you haven't seen his movies, they're are amazing. And when it comes to the amazing works of Frank Henenlotter, most people play favoritism to the *Basket Case* series. I mean, there were three of them, and that series really went the most mainstream. *Basket Case 3* was produced by 20th Century Fox, so it was more in the public eye. Or many people fell in love with *Frankenhooker*. I mean really, who couldn't love that title? Even his more recent fare, *Bad Biology* is pretty out there. BUT, with all this said, the film with the special place in my heart is *Brain Damage*.

Brain Damage is the quintessential '80s ultra-gore extravaganza. It shows that horror can be fun and freaky. I remember the first time I saw this film, I was enchanted. I've seen it 50+ times by now, ha ha. It's seriously one of the most fun films I've ever seen. Amazing gore, crazy visuals and a fun monster that sings! It's such a strange and unique concept, unbelievably trippy, and features one of my all time favorite kill scenes: death by alien blowjob. You have to see it to understand lol. Aylmer is hilarious. Seriously, one of the best and most adorable villains with razor sharp teeth ever. It's just pure fun and also still not on enough people's radars, so you can always turn on your friends to a new film they haven't heard of. It's become that film that I like to keep in my back pocket to recommend to friends that are looking for a fun horror movie.

Frank really does horror different than any other filmmaker. His voice is just so different and strange compared to the voices of most. He's always marched to the beat of his own drum.

Because of his brilliance and unwavering individualism, I dedicated the first feature film I ever made, *My Pure Joy*, to the works of Frank Henenlotter because of this bad ass movie and all the advice and kindness he's given me anytime I've reached out over the years. Frank is not only an amazing talent, but a great guy.

CREATURE FROM THE BLACK LAGOON

BY
TODD ROBEY

Artist, Visual Arts Instructor
RobeyArt.com
Instagram/Twitter: @RobeyArt
Facebook: @TheArtOfToddRobey

I believe the year was 1976 or 1977…I was around 5 or 6 years old, and I can't remember if I was home from school one day watching TV or if it was on "The Family Film Festival" on a Sunday afternoon after *Popeye* cartoons, but whichever it was, that is when I saw my FIRST monster movie, *The Creature from the Black Lagoon*!!! (duh duh duuhhhhh) I very much remember three things from that first monster movie experience:

1. I wasn't scared of the creature for some reason.

2. I couldn't understand why the men were trying to kill the creature because he only wanted a friend to swim with.

3. I really, really, REALLY thought the creature's webbed claws

were super cool and I wondered what it'd be like to swim with those hands...

Very shortly after seeing this movie, I went for a day's adventure with my family to the Enchanted Village in Buena Park, CA. I remember walking across the Bridge of Enchantment into the park with my mom, sister, Aunt and 4 cousins, and first thing on our agenda we went to see *The Island of Dr. Moreau Stunt Show*! All I remember from this animal stunt show was a guy in a bad gorilla suit throwing another Tarzan-like guy off a huge treehouse and into the lagoon below. Once he splashed down into the water, you guessed it...along comes my hero, the Creature from the Black Lagoon! The Creature swam up to Tarzan, grabbed him with his awesome claws and dragged him under water. Then I saw a very big squish of red paint, I mean blood, flow out in the dark, murky water, and Tarzan was gone. My mom reassured me it wasn't real and that Tarzan was ok, but now I wasn't so sure about this Creature guy and I remembered being very wary as we exited the theater, filing past the lagoon water tank. Later in the day, my family and I rode the Tana River Raft ride. Little did I know this would be the encounter I'd never forget! That Enchanted Village experience burned the Creature into my brain forever! We rode the boring river raft ride, all 8 of us crammed into a black, rubber, zodiac raft with a small outboard engine and driver. I sat in the back of the raft near the driver, next to my mom and sister, with my cousin Greg across from me. At the turn around point of the ride, we entered a dark water cave, and yep!... you guessed it, right in the middle of that cave, from under the water comes the Creature up onto the side of the boat!!! A couple things happened very quickly here...my whole family erupted into hysterical screaming and, being that the Creature was on my cousin's side of the boat, he jumped away, knocking me off my bench and into the fuel can and then over the side of the raft! Now this was early '70s amusement park rides kids, so there were no safety rails or seat belts, just the rubber edge of the 10-man raft and the Black Lagoon beyond...

Luckily, the boat driver grabbed me by my sweatshirt quickly and kept me from going all the way over. Instead, my head and arm only got wet, but that was enough to petrify me with fear! As I was hauled back into the boat, my back hurting from the fuel tank, and my head and sweatshirt sleeve soaking wet, I looked over to see the those amazingly cool, webbed claws with the broken fingernails resting on the side of the boat, as the Creature continued to taunt and scare my already hysterical family. We exited the cave with most of the kids crying, my mom soothing my screaming sister, and I think my aunt was even yelling at the boat driver. As we headed back towards the dock away from the water cave, I never took my eyes off that Creature. I watched his every move fearing the worst, still petrified from my near-death experience...and then he waved at me!!! He waved at me from the water and immediately my fear melted away! I smiled and frantically waved back with my soaked sweatshirt sleeve flopping around, my faith restored in my monster hero! As soon as we were back on the dock, I was asking if we could go again, hoping the next time I wouldn't be so afraid and maybe I could touch his awesome claws...but, as I'm sure you can guess, I was met with a resounding "HELL NO!" from the rest of my family.

Since that fateful sighting so shortly after seeing the movie, I have never been able to shake my love for the Creature! From doing just about every water sport known to man, working as an ocean lifeguard in Huntington Beach, swimming for hours and hours in my friend Jeff's pool all summer long wearing his *Creature from the Black Lagoon* swim set (green fins, headpiece with built in goggles & the awesome claw/hand paddle gloves), I have always thought about the Creature. I've even somehow transferred that monster love to my son, also his first monster movie, and his most beloved bath tub toy growing up was a little rubber *Creature from the Black Lagoon* figure I bought at the grocery store around Halloween for a dollar. To this day, his favorite painting I've done is a multi-media, 3-D piece named *The Creature Stole My Surfboard* which hangs in his bedroom and I'm not allowed to sell. By my count, I think I've completed about 10 different art pieces inspired by the Creature, the latest having been delivered to gallery about a month from writing this. So, it would be a huge understatement to say the *Creature from the Black Lagoon* is one of my favorite horror movies from a VERY young age. The Creature has greatly influenced my life, my art and my love of monsters, and could arguably be considered my spirit animal.

AN AMERICAN WEREWOLF IN LONDON

BY
TERRY WOLFINGER

Character Designer/Concept Artist/Illustrator
Jurassic Park 2, Michael Jackson's Ghosts, Terminator 3,
The Suffering Video Game,
Famous Monsters of Filmland Magazine
Wolfinger.BigCartel.com
Facebook: @Terry.Wolfinger   Instagram: @TerryWolfinger

Growing up as a kid, I was not always a fan of horror movies. I did like the classics, like Boris Karloff's *Frankenstein*, Bela Lugosi's *Dracula*, Chaney's *Phantom*, and *Creature From the Black Lagoon*, to name a few. There was coolness to those films and characters - a creepy other-worldliness to them, but not necessarily terrifying. Most of the other horror movies from the '70s, like *The Exorcist*, actually did terrify me and I didn't really enjoy the experience. It was partly because I had a very vivid imagination and those films took on a reality all their own. Those movies would plague me weeks and weeks after seeing them. I also had an older brother who loved to torment me about that fact and would taunt me with scariest images he could find from his monster magazines or subject me to watching the late night creature feature that he would promise wasn't scary at all. Though, they did play a lot of *Godzilla* movies and Ray Harryhausen classics, which I loved.

The movie that changed all that for me was John Landis' *An American Werewolf in London*. I saw it as a double feature with *Heavy Metal* at this little theater near my house when I was about 13 or 14. The theater was sandwiched between this impossibly narrow space between our grocery store, a Chinese restaurant, and other small shops. I went to the late show with my brother and one of his friends and was mostly excited to see *Heavy Metal*, as I was also really into animation and drawing at the time. *Heavy Metal* played first, which was a fun, crazy, weird little movie. A brief intermission and bathroom break, and we are back in our seats. The lights go down and the crackle of the soundtrack starts playing Bobby Vinton's version of "Blue Moon" and sets a nice relaxing tone against shots of the English countryside. And it totally disarms you from what's about to come.

American Werewolf was the first horror movie I saw that had a lot of humor woven into the story. And the humor came from the situations - "a naked American man stole my balloons" - not just inserted jokes or one-liners. The two main characters, David and Jack, are instantly likable, which also makes their ultimate situation all the more suspenseful and tragic. You know one of or both of these guys are doomed from the start. All the supporting characters are fantastic, as well as the writing, directing and Rick Baker's state-of-the-art makeup effects. The scary parts are truly terrifying, and for me, made being scared fun for the first time. Seeing the first reveal of Jack after the werewolf attack, with his slashed face and gash in his neck with his trachea hanging out was both horrific and hilarious at the same time. From that day on, everything in my sketchbooks had their throats torn out (everything from *Garfield* to *E.T.*, to whatever jackass happened to bully me that week).

Everyone in the theater was having a blast too. When David's transformation scene came on, we were all just mesmerized, as if it was actually happening. The coolest, freakiest thing I had ever seen. I loved it. And the whole "dream-within-a-dream" sequence - I don't know if John Landis was the first to come up with that idea, but it was the first time I had ever seen anything like that and it scared the crap out of me! Laughing through the screams or screaming through the laughs, these are just a few of the reasons why *An American Werewolf in London* is my favorite horror movie of all time. It's one of the few that has withstood the test of time. It still holds up, and I watch it at least once a year. And so, my friends, in closing, stay on the road, keep clear of the moors, and beware the moon.

PUPPET MASTER
BY
JULIA HAPNEY

Special Makeup Effects Artist/Puppeteer
Zombeavers, VHS/Viral, The Summoners,
The Basement, Snake Outta Compton
Facebook: @EvilDreamer
JuliaHapney.com

One of my favorite films is and will always be *Puppet Master*...actually the entire *Puppet Master* series (*1* to *Retro* to be specific).

I was around seven or eight years old when I first watched *Puppet Master,* and I immediately fell in love with all of the puppet characters (Blade being my favorite because he is just so badass! I also think this is why I love Judge Doom so much in *Roger Rabbit* - they look kinda similar). I have been a horror fan my entire life; a passion that I luckily turned into a lifestyle as an adult. I was diagnosed with Crohn's disease in 1993 (age 9), and because of that, I was home sick a lot and watched movie after movie to take my mind off the pain. I grew up in a small town on the border of Ohio/West Virginia and we had one local independent video store called Network Video. Lucky for me, it was next to the grocery store. While my parents went grocery shopping, they would give me a five dollar bill and I would go to the video store and examine every VHS cover in the horror section, over and over. Five dollars would get me a new release and two classic movies. Everything I rented was from the horror section (my mom signed a release allowing me to rent whatever I wanted), so by the time I was 10, I had literally watched every horror film in the store. I am so thankful for Network Video because they carried all the cool independent horror films. Well, all except for *Puppet Master 2* (they had *1*, and *3*...and then later *4* and *5*...but never *2*).

I was determined to see *Puppet Master 2*. My sister, Kristina, helped me call all the other video stores in towns that were an hour away, until we finally found one that carried it! My amazing mother (who got me into horror in the first place... and watched every single horror movie with me over and over) drove all the way to the video store to rent me *Puppet Master 2*. We never returned the movie, and I still own that exact copy on VHS. I actually still have every VHS (*1-5*) that I owned as a kid. I also owned them all individually on DVD when they were released and I later purchased the DVD box set (it was out of print for a very long time due to some sort of legal situation, and I spent years trying to acquire it). Then, the day finally came when I got to meet Charles Band at a horror convention in 2006 - literally on 6/6/06. I waited around for hours for him to come back to the Full Moon table for the chance to meet him and have him sign it. When he finally arrived, I remember trying to stop shaking because I was so nervous. He was so friendly and nice, and so happy to hear that I was such a fan of his films. I couldn't believe I was in the presence of the guy that made all this magic come to life!!! It was a bucket list moment for sure.

My favorite thing about *Puppet Master* are the puppets themselves. There are so many puppets!!! Throughout the series, we learn all about each puppet and their backstory (who they were designed after, the soul in each doll, how they came to life, how they died, who they loved, hated, feared etc.). Each is very different in every way!!! There is Leech Woman (who spits out leeches to suck the blood of her victims), Blade (Leader of the puppets, with his white hair, black hat, black coat, a knife, a hook for hands, and a ghostly white skeletal face), Tunneler (who digs into people with his drill-like headpiece), Pinhead (who has human-sized arms, a tiny pinhead, and is the muscle of the group - he often strangles his victims or holds them down so the other puppets can attack), and Jester (has a 3-part movable face that changes from happy to anger, sadness, etc. He is the puppet who kills the least but that doesn't mean he isn't involved in the murders). Other favorites that came along later include Torch, Six Shooter, and even Faust and Hitler make puppet appearances in the series. The puppets go from being the good guys to the bad guys and back again. They often protect the humans of the films, and towards the end of the series, it becomes an all out puppet war...but that's not until after the audience learns all about the Egyptian spell that animates them, as well as traveling back in time to Nazi Germany, where most of the main puppets were created. There is so much influence from real history showcased within these films, it really brought the story of the puppets to life, and it also made me interested in learning about real historical events as a kid, (specifically the Holocaust, Egyptian legends, and magic, like the Book of the Dead).

As much as I loved the films, I always looked forward to watching the *VideoZone* behind-the-scenes specials that played after the credits rolled. These videos showed special clips of the FX people/puppeteers making, working, and playing with the puppets. I remember thinking how cool THAT job must be! I didn't realize that I could have that kind of job until many years later.

My first working interaction with an FX artist connected to these films was with an amazing guy named Jeff Farley.

While I was working under him at his shop on *Universal Soldier 4* and *Return of the Killer Shrews*, he told me many stories of his *Puppet Master* days. When our show wrapped, he gifted me a Blade head from one of the original molds. I still get excited every time I hold that head. One of these days, I will get around to fabricating the rest of him. I will always be thankful for all of the stories Jeff shared with me, as well as my Blade head.

A few years later, while working for Mark Rappaport (owner of Creature Effects) on *The Lone Ranger* and *Zombeavers*, he gifted me Pinhead and little Hitler puppet heads from his original molds...and I was told even more amazing stories from the set!! Mark is such a great guy!! It is so amazing to hear the stories of the guys who made my favorite puppets come to life. It was a lot of work for them, but they really had a lot of fun making all the magic happen!!!

After repeatedly viewing these films as a kid, I remember wishing my Barbie and Lee Middleton dolls would come to life. Before I went to sleep, I would set my dolls up in a specific way, hoping to find that they had moved when I woke up. Sadly, they never came to life (that I know of), but I still have hope that one day they will!

I look forward to the day I get to show these films to my niece Eleni. Before she was born, I purchased her first puppet, her first Barbie, and her first Monster High doll (a small introduction to horror) and gifted them to her at her baby shower. The *Puppet Master* series has been a wonderful story that has stayed in my heart for over 25 years. I can't wait to share the magical world Charles Band and the many FX artists and puppeteers created, to see the expression on her face and in her eyes when she meets some of my oldest and dearest little friends.

Sweet Dreams and Pleasant Nightmares!
xoxo, Julia Hapney

FRANKENSTEIN
MEETS THE WOLFMAN

BY
C. COURTNEY JOYNER

Author/Screenwriter/Film Historian
Nemo Rising, Shotgun, From a Whisper To a Scream,
Class of 1999, Puppet Master III: Toulon's Revenge
CCourtneyJoyner.com
Facebook: @CCourtney.Joyner

T he problem is, the reeling mind. I think about the little kid in his pajamas, staying up to watch Dr. Shock on Channel 17, and all those Universal Monsters embracing, and chasing me, while Hammer, Amicus, and Eddie Romero horrors played at our local drive-in.

A downtown Philly kiddie-matinee let me discover *Mysterious Island* in re-release after my buddy and I snuck into *Mark of the Devil* across the street. Captain Nemo didn't need a vomit bag, but I still had mine stuffed in my pocket, watching Harryhausen's glorious animations.

But a favorite horror movie? Not the scariest, or most influential, but favorite. Somehow it always comes back to one film, out of thousands; the love is spread that super-thin. But this single film, its monsters, and a cardboard box, were the first to capture my geek-soul.

Frankenstein Meets the Wolfman. There's the hint of memory that I actually held the Castle Films 8mm box before seeing the movie; the image of the Lugosi monster struggling with Chaney's transformed Talbot absolutely hypnotizing in color. This was also around the time of *Famous Monsters* #42, with Ron Cobb's amazing mash-up cover, combining an almost Frazetta-like brush interpretation of the images from the one-sheet. Forry Ackerman promised, "The world will explode when Frankenstein meets the Wolfman!"

Not the world, but my eight-year old heart, as I finally saw the film on *Scream-In*, and watched what is still the single, most terrifying moment in the Universal Monster cycle: Larry Talbot's resurrection in the crypt. That was fifty years ago, and God only knows how many times I've seen that moment since, and it still kills me. The poetry of Roy William Neill's seamless, gliding direction, powered over-the-top by the incredible Hans Salter music sting when graverobber Cyril Delevanti is grabbed by the hand with the fingernails.

No explanations – just horror. And it's perfect.

And that scene is only one of the films glories: Lon Chaney never looked better in a film during his Universal contract days. Fighting trim and double-breasted, he's a coiled lycanthropic spring. And when he's transformed, the Wolfman scenes in the film are the best treatment of the character ever, with Jack Pierce refining the look to a fierce glory.

The performances are so solid and elevated, and Ilona Massey is the stuff of horror fantasy; frankly, she scorches it. As does George Robinson, whose photography is stunning in its detail; and amazing use of shadow, combined beautifully with the miniature work that culminates in that great, slow-motion dynamiting of the dam.

Lugosi's monster? I've always loved it. Yes, we know about the scenes that were cut, and the lack of explanation for his awkward blindness, but we understand because we've all seen *The Ghost of Frankenstein*. For any monster kid, it's not a problem; not knowing the history of the monster is like denying the sound of a neighbor's dog. It's familiar, and a part of us.

Frankenstein Meets the Wolfman has often been the target of finger-wagging aficionados, who decry the movie as the start of the Universal "monster rallies," and the downfall of the classic monster cycle. Frankly, they're petrified in their own ice. It isn't *The Bride of Frankenstein* or *The Black Cat*, and isn't supposed to be.

Frankenstein Meets the Wolfman isn't the downfall, it's the collective of everything that wonderful fantasy world of Universal Horror really meant to any kid who lost themselves in those black and white images – a simple, and beautiful escape.

The scariest, or most important? No.

The favorite? Always.

DAY OF THE DEAD

BY
CHRIS HAMPTON

Make-Up FX Artist
Passion of the Christ, The Curious Case of Benjamin Button,
The Watchmen, Cabin in the Woods, The Hobbit,
Fear the Walking Dead
Instagram: @CJH1313

What more does a kid need to see walking around a video store in the '80s? I had to see this movie. My parents would let me watch some horror movies back then, but nothing like this. I was already a big fan of *Jaws* and *Creature from the Black Lagoon* (basically the older classics), but there were so many VHS box covers luring me into movies I was dying to see but couldn't. Luckily, my older cousins would let me watch all the movies I couldn't see at home when I would spend my summers with them. The *Dead* films were definitely next on my list.

There are plenty of other horror films I could have written about. Some, I feel, are much better in areas as important films to the genre, though none have made me think the way George Romero got me to think. Sadly, as I write this, I just heard of his passing.

R.I.P. George A. Romero

Night, *Dawn*, and *Day of the Dead* brought a real human element to horror. They each illustrate a social commentary that still holds up decades later, not to mention, they started one of the biggest subgenres in film, paving the way for shows like *The Walking Dead* and one of the best books I've read, *World War Z* (the book only!). As much as they are zombie films, what makes them sit deeper with me is that the dead are more of icing on the cake, second to the human condition. These films showed that in face of the constant reminder of what's inevitably next, a more primal darkness comes into play: the human mind. The dead bring out something that's inherent in all of us. Some become sadistic, paranoid or terrified, while others rise to the occasion as heroes. Unless you end up surrounded by a horde, most die from the choice of either another person or a mental collapse. It brought so many opportunities for complex characters. Those films would have me thinking all the time about what some random people stuck in other places would be going through. I obviously wasn't the only one, since most every zombie film follows the same rules that were established in the original, just with new characters and different scenarios.

Each film in the trilogy has reasons to make my consideration for a favorite, but *Day of the Dead* had more of an impact on where I'm at today. From the opening scene showing Dr. Tongue emerging from a sun flare, to the finale, where everyone is being torn apart, there were so many gags and FX going on throughout the whole film, I couldn't believe what I was seeing. The makeup FX in *Day of the Dead* were next level. What Tom Savini and his crew accomplished started a whole new generation of FX artists. KNB and Optic Nerve were born out of that crew and have been among the leaders in the industry ever since. They introduced the most memorable and iconic zombie in Bub, created by the late John Vulich, one of the founders of Optic Nerve. It was that film and those artists that created the modern zombie, setting a new standard in the genre. I've been lucky to have worked with KNB on a couple projects, including *Fear the Walking Dead.* Getting to take a small part in that history is something I never would have thought back in that old video store, but apparently my mom did.

As a kid, all I wanted to do was be an actor and tell stories. I would create characters and mess with people every chance I could. I would also write stories about the different characters I wanted to play. I used to steal my mom's makeup and make wounds or other gore effects just to try and trick people. My mom always reminds me about the time I broke knife handles off and glued them to myself, then poured whatever makeshift blood I could come up with all over and laid against the front door waiting for her to get home to find my body. It didn't go over well, but I would keep trying things to get people to freak out. My friends would go home after I would do makeups on them with latex stuck in their hair or clothes stained with fake blood. We even had some people call the police on us for faking getting hit by a car. It was always a mess and a lot of fun. She would say, "You love those horror movies and doing the FX stuff. You should be an FX artist." But I didn't think twice about it. Those FX things were only to make my characters more real. But she was right.

After high school, I was working construction, still doing FX, watching horror films, and writing stories in my spare time. The job we were on got into some trouble, which put me out of work and broke. I was fed up with being a carpenter and looked into some schools for music or acting. One day, looking through a *Fangoria* magazine, I saw what looked like the old Tom Savini *Scream Greats* ad, but it was an ad for a new FX school he was planning on opening. I brought this up to my mom and she said of course, "I told you so!" A couple months later, I was in Pittsburgh, home to the *Dead* films, taking part in what most of us from that first wave call the test group of the school; definitely learning, but mainly practicing and trying to keep our sanity living in the tiny coal town. I had come full circle without even realizing it. There I was, going to all the locations the films were shot, working with some of the same artists that worked on the films, and working with Tom himself for most of my time there. They were stressful times, but the memories I'll never forget. I made friends and colleagues that are still in my life today. From a cool cover of a VHS tape 15 years before, to working with the same people who sparked that fire.

Since starting makeup FX professionally back around 2001, I've been able to take part in all kinds of projects, but the ones that always comes back around are zombies, and right now they seem to be bigger than ever. Every producer or director has their own version of what they want to see, though none have really been as effective as the original in my opinion. While the FX have evolved, the stories have held the test of time and left the door wide open to possible ideas. These have kept myself and many other artists busy making a career out of the dead.

I probably would have always loved horror films, but I don't know if I would have become an artist in the FX industry had I not read that one tagline. Because of this, I've been able to travel the world and work on some great projects with amazing people, some of which I've admired most of my life. Going back to that day in the video store, I guess my path in life originated from the dead.

THE ROCKY HORROR PICTURE SHOW

BY
SPOOKY DAN WALKER

Producer/Writer/Director/Horror Culture Activist
Slay Belles, The Devil's Carnival,
Alleluia! The Devil's Carnival
Instagram: @SpookyDanWalker
Twitter/Facebook: @SpookyDan

As a teenager, I loved trying to win radio call-in contests. You know, "be the 10th caller" when you hear whatever song and win free tickets to a movie or concert. This was pre-cell phone days, so I had the phone programmed to speed dial the radio station, and for about a year, I kept winning tickets to screenings of various films; *Aliens*, *Poltergeist II*, or *Top Gun*. Whatever movie it was, I didn't care. I loved film, so I would drag my dad with me to all of them. One of the contests was for a screening of some crappy comedy (maybe *Crocodile Dundee*? I don't recall). This particular screening happened to be a midnight movie at the local cinema next-door to the (then thriving) Woodland Mall in Grand Rapids Michigan. This theatre also happened to be playing other midnight movies, and I remember seeing a cast of characters out front in costumes, having fun…and being freaks. I didn't know what it was all about. All I knew was that I was mesmerized, intrigued, and slightly scared of what I saw. At one point during my movie, I left to pee, and the same group of weirdos were still in the lobby long after midnight, changing costumes and still looking like they were at a party. I needed to know what this thing was.

Later, I learned what this thing was: *The Rocky Horror Picture Show*. I knew it was a gay, horror musical - and a full-on freak show happened anywhere that it played. I think I was 12 years old when I first went with a group of friends to actually see it. None of us had any idea what the movie was, we just knew they threw toast and rice and sang along. When I sat down, the freak show was in full force. They wanted to know which of us was a virgin…we all lied. But then, this magical movie came across the screen, with music that was infectious, with visuals like no other, and a cast that seemed to know just how absurd it was, but didn't care. In one night, I went from mesmerized to full-on obsessed. I needed to know more. I bought the vinyl audience participation album, the book, and even signed up for the snail mail fan club. Within a few months, my bedroom was decorated with posters and flyers for it. The lousy part was that my parents would not allow me to go see it. It was a midnight movie, way past my curfew. I conned them into letting me go the first couple times, but after that, midnight movies and *Rocky Horror* were off limits. Like every rebellious teenager, this just fueled the fire to become even more obsessed. So, every Friday night, I would sneak out my bedroom window to see *Rocky*. After a couple of months, one of the cast members asked me to be *Rocky* in the shadow cast, not because I was ripped, but because I had blonde hair. So, I became the stand-by Rocky for a few dozen shows. Week after week, I would sneak out and go to the movie and occasional afterparties. This movie wasn't just a movie, it was a lifestyle. It was weird and gay, but the best part was being a 13-year-old straight boy surrounded by girls in lingerie. In playing Rocky, my "job" was to act out the scene to the song "Touch-a Touch-a Touch-a Touch Me," where I had to fake feel up this cute, short, gothic, busty girl named Francheska! She was probably 17 and always made me feel her up for real! Again, I was 13, so this was basically heaven on earth.

The party ended a year or so later when my parents caught me sneaking out, and it ended the pseudo-coming-of-age period where *Rocky* was more about boobs than the film itself. By the time I was in college, I had seen it around 70 times in a theater. Then, it finally came out on VHS and I saved up $95 to buy my very own copy of the film, which I then watched about a million times. The thing is, when you really pay attention to *Rocky Horror*, it's a strange movie that doesn't always make sense, but something deeper is happening than what is inherently on the surface. There is the community (which I will get back to), but the film's direction and acting has something otherworldly about it. Something magical is happening inside the film and it's hard to put your finger on why. Murder, incest, transvestites, and singing; this should not be a movie that can change the actual lives of so many people, but it does just that. The style is so over the top, from the production design to the costumes to the tiny details inside the castle. They all reek of low budget, but somehow never quite feel low budget.

When you watch a movie dozens of times, regardless of the movie, you start to notice small things. You notice the details. As someone who always aspired to make movies as a career, studying a film so intensely teaches you a lot about filmmaking. The acting, stage direction, editing, and pacing all became a mini film school. I then read more about the behind the scenes shenanigans in a variety of *Rocky Horror* books, and it showed me that even with a bizarre film concept like *Rocky Horror*, a story needs to be told, and if told in an entertaining way, it will find an audience. In the case of *Rocky Horror*, the audience was a living breathing part of the film.

You can't really talk about *Rocky Horror* without talking about the community that embraced it. Allow me to go on a brief tangent. In the 1980s, being gothic, punk or unique was not the norm. Being gay was still very taboo and looking like an alien punk rocker from Mars was only for New York socialites and rock stars. At that time in Midwest Michigan, there were more churches than gas stations, and any god-fearing Christian wasn't a very good Christian if you were allowing these freaks to (gasp) be freaks. The sexuality in *Rocky Horror* forced people out of their comfort zones, and encouraged you to be open to all sorts of people. Be a freak within this community and you will be embraced. Skinny, fat, hot or ugly didn't matter at *Rocky Horror*. You are SUPPOSED TO let your personal freak flag fly. My freak flag was of the gothic variety, and us goth kids looked pretty normal at a *Rocky Horror* show. The community was and still is all about love and acceptance.

When the time came to make my first feature, I decided to make a Christmas horror film called *Slay Belles* and needed an actor to play Santa Claus. I went after 2 people: Tim Curry and Barry Bostwick. Many other names had been suggested, because they would bring in more sales or were more famous, but they never mattered to me. I wanted my first movie to include someone who was royalty to me. Tim Curry's health had fallen, so I never formally approached him, but I did chase Barry Bostwick until he said yes. I am happy to say that Barry Bostwick, better known as Brad Majors ("ASSHOLE" to the *Rocky* fans,) is my Santa Claus, and he steals the movie! And even better, he is now my friend.

For a gothic kid from the Midwest, *Rocky Horror* has influenced my life in countless ways, but what it did that was so important was teach me the craft of making a movie that matters to an audience, and to embrace that audience when it responds. As someone who lives and breathes horror films, one of the things that's most important to me to embrace our horror community. The horror community (like the *Rocky Horror* community) is a rabid group of people from all walks of life that wants to be entertained. You can go to any horror convention in any country and witness firsthand a community of loving and accepting people who encourage each other to let their freak flags fly. To this day, as a 44-year-old man, I still have *Rocky Horror* posters on the walls of my home.

*Some of you reading this may argue that *The Rocky Horror Picture Show* isn't a true horror film, and you are correct. But it does have many of the required horror tropes. Plus, any Google search for the word "horror" brings up a ton of *Rocky Horror* results.

JOHN CARPENTER'S THE THING

BY
KEN JACOBSEN

Film & Video Game Composer/Music Producer
The Amazing Spiderman (VG), Monday Night Football
Metallica's Ride The Lighting, Hell's Belles, Mania
Facebook/Instagram: @KenJacobsenMusic
Twitter: @KenCJacobsen

I'm not sure if I would consider this essay about my favorite horror movie as much as it is about one movie that inspired me early on, shaping my attitude towards horror and sci-fi.

The first horror movies that influenced me were made by John Carpenter (*Halloween*, *The Fog*, *They Live*). But the one that really spoke to me was *The Thing*, based on a book by John W. Campbell, with an abundance of references to author H.P. Lovecraft (one of my favorite horror authors). It was also a remake of a '50s movie by the same name that I also was into.

John Carpenter scored his own movies until this one. *The Thing* was the first where he decided to get help scoring, hiring established composer Ennio Morricone, who has always been

one of the most iconic and daring composers. As a film composer, I've always been fan of his. In this instance, he manages
to capture the signature style of Carpenter's particular brand of
simple, but effective iconic synthesizer scores, as well as adding
an orchestra for added dimension to the sound.

The movie is set in the stark, isolated, and cold tundra of
the Antarctic, with 2 scientific outposts; one manned by Americans and one manned by Norwegians, separated by a distance
an hour by helicopter. We witness the mysterious chase of a
dog over the frozen tundra by a helicopter, culminating with
the dog running into the American station. Due to the desperate actions of the Norwegian team to kill the dog, they ultimately get killed themselves. However, the dog survives. Since
this sequence of events puzzles the Americans, they decide to
investigate the Norwegian station. Here, they find complete
devastation and clues of what turns out to be a "the find of the
century". This discovery, as it turns out, is an alien spaceship
with an empty ice sarcophagus and a mysterious carcass of a
distorted humanoid monstrosity. They bring the carcass back
to base. Through science, they discover that this is an imitation
trying to appear human. The scientist in charge realizes the
consequences to the entire world and commences a destruction
of vital communications and any way of escape. They appre-
hend and isolate him in an outhouse. They consequently put
the escaped dog in the pound with the rest of the dogs as it was
roaming mysteriously around the station. Once they put the
dog in the pound, we find out the true horror and truth about
him. It starts a gory metamorphosis, getting caught mid-act
by the dog handler. An alert is issued and the men gather to
witness this grotesque spectacle. As they torch the entity, they
realize that anyone could now be The Thing and they wouldn't
know it. Fear and suspicion becomes the emotional backbone
of the movie. The Thing slowly builds its particular brand of
terror, all while the systematic burning of the remains of the
various incarnations of the alien occurs. In the meantime, our
main hero, Mac, gains command of the station due to an in-

cident involving a sabotaged experiment to identify the imposter. Since there is doubt about the key access to their blood supplies, and the station leader is the sole owner of that key, he decides to relinquish his role as leader to Mac.

After witnessing a botched resurrection, (culminating in the station doctors' gruesome death), they have no doubts about the horror facing them. As the tension builds between the crew members, Mac asserts control after being left out in the cold. He conducts a test with blood samples to determine who is an imposter. After tying everyone to a couch, one tests positive and transforms. They burn the creature and decide to check on the scientist they locked up in the shed, only to find that he escaped. They discover a loose floorboard and a subterranean room. There, they find a spaceship under construction and destroy it. They search for the doctor while setting charges to destroy the entire station, during which, a few more men gets absorbed by the entity. Now, Mac is alone to blow up the camp and The Thing. He manages to escape and crawl out in the snow, where he meets Childs, who had gotten lost in the night. As the camp is ablaze, they realize that this is the end.

As far as the score is concerned, Morricone perfectly captured the essence of the stark coldness and the fear involved, delivering examples of Carpenter's signature sound while still retaining his own personality and expertise.

Although the special effects of *The Thing* are primitive by today's standard, Carpenter remains a master of the horror genre. The 2012 prequel doesn't manage to capture the tension, fear, and vibe from the 1982 version. The 1951 *The Thing from Another World* is a much different version altogether, embodying the spirit of the B-movie era. But *John Carpenter's The Thing* is one of the classic horror/sci-fi movies of all time.

CREEPSHOW
BY
JARED RIVET

Screenwriter/Actor/Director/Producer/Host
Jackals, Earbud Theater, Dead Right Horror Trivia
Twitter: @JaredRivet1
Facebook: @Jared.Rivet
Instagram: @ScribeJR

"The Most Fun You'll Ever Have Being Scared!" was the tagline and this was an extremely seductive lure for an 11-year-old only child who was obsessed with – but terrified by – horror movies. Since I was too young to see *Creepshow* in the theater when it came out in the fall of 1982, I didn't get to see it until it was released on home video in 1983. I had very young parents that were extremely lax with their parental concerns over the kinds of things I watched (not to mention it was a different era and the attitude in general about these things was a little more fluid back then). They were definitely into genre cinema (nowhere near as much as I was), and we would go to the theater and/or rent VHS tapes like crazy back then and watch them together. Mostly sci-fi and horror. And horror was coincidentally in the midst of a golden age at that particular moment, and a young impressionable mind like mine couldn't help but be warped and inspired by the glut of horror and fantasy films flowing into theaters and onto television in vast numbers.

Full confession: horror movies actually scared me back then. Really scared me. Nightmares for days…if I could manage to even fall asleep since I was usually too terrified by whatever my imagination had conjured up that might be hiding in the closet or under the bed or lurking in the shadows outside my bedroom door. And still, I was drawn to horror films and scary stories like a moth to a flame, and I actively sought them out, but when things got really suspenseful or especially scary, I was predictably traumatized. (My father could tell you how high I jumped into the air before landing in his lap in the theater when Robbie's clown doll popped up behind him in that Cuesta Verde bedroom in the third act of the PG-rated *Poltergeist* in 1982.) I'm not sure what that says about the childhood version of me as a person, but I must have loved being scared because I kept going back for more.

Which brings me back to "The Most Fun You'll Ever Have Being Scared!" and *Creepshow*. I was already enjoying a steady diet of horror films by the time *Creepshow* came along and I knew I wanted to grow up to make movies (*Star Wars* had taken care of that). I already knew who Stephen King was (I had already seen the adaptations of *The Shining, Carrie* and *Salem's Lot*, and yes, they scared the living shit out of me) but I am not sure that I knew who George A. Romero was.

But all of that changed the fateful day we rented *Creepshow* on VHS and slapped it into the old Philco VCR. In fact, a lot of things changed that day.

How do you encapsulate the experience of watching a movie that changes your life? I don't know if I can, but *Creepshow* did it for me in spades. There was something about the set-up, with Tom Atkins' abusive dad mercilessly throwing away Billy's comic books, and then the ominously whimsical, EC Comics-inspired, animated opening credit sequence that let me know that this was indeed going to be the most fun I ever had being scared. And it was.

Yes, it was scary, but there was a winking reassurance to it all. It was scary, but ol' George wasn't going to traumatize me. He wanted to take me on a scary ride, one full of color and mood and fun, one that I could not only survive unscathed but that I might want to go on again and again. I fell in love with the anthology format that day: five stories?? Five different scary stories?? I can remember being bowled over when one ended and the next one began. It happened so many times that I didn't want it to end. In fact, when grumpy Tom Atkins shows up again at the end, grumbling at the breakfast table about his stiff neck, I would have been absolutely fine if a sixth story began about that. And each one instantly burned itself into my psyche. Starting right with the snooty rich family of "Father's Day," with crazy Aunt Bedelia, dancing Ed Harris, and the greatest zombie-rising-from-the-grave sequence I had ever seen. The sheer repetition of corpse Nathan Grantham's line "Where's my cake?" had us giggling in hysterics. The gore was thrilling, the comic panel transitions and lighting effects were game-changing, something I had never seen before. And the music! A mix of modern, Carpenter-esque synth from composer John Harrison alternating with old school library tracks from '50s and '60s sci-fi/horror films that charmed the hell out of me. I wanted, nay, needed that music in my life.

Old Nate gives us a ghoulishly funny, final jump scare, carrying Aunt Sylvia's head in on a platter for all to see, adorned with lit birthday candles and his satisfied utterance of "It's Father's Day…and I got my cake" and then we're off to meet poor, lonely Jordy Verrill.

I remember initially finding the tonal shift a bit jarring from "Father's Day" to "Jordy," especially since "Father's Day" seemed to be not only paying such a committed homage to

EC Comics tropes but also to the popular slasher films of the then-current era (a tragic act of wrongdoing years before leads directly to the return of the wronged in the present day, who then stalks those he feels are responsible, killing them one-by-one in gorily shocking ways). "The Lonesome Death of Jordy Verrill" felt like an exceedingly goofy detour, that is, until the tragically inevitable ending, followed immediately by the radio announcer's unconsciously portentous declaration that "lots of rain" is in the weather forecast. But Stephen King's unbelievable performance (especially his singular reading of the now famous line "Meteor shit!") won me over, and the final fate of this poor, country bumpkin certainly struck me with its stealthy shift into pathos.

I remember feeling like "Something to Tide You Over" might be my favorite story as I watched (it held that mantle for all of 25 minutes), with Leslie Nielsen and Ted Danson's great interplay, along with the escalation of Richard Vicker's elaborately planned revenge. I loved how Danson's Harry Wentworth didn't know that the plan started before Richard even showed up at his door.

The fiendishly elaborate buried-up-to-your-neck drowning while being filmed for posterity, Nielsen's gleefully malevolent performance, and the waterlogged zombies back for ironic revenge (and their black, watery bullet wounds) had me completely hooked.

If that had been all there was, I would have been perfectly satisfied. But "Tide" ended and, to my delight, right around the one-hour mark, we comic-panel-transitioned to another story. This one was called "The Crate." And not only did it turn out to be the centerpiece of the movie, the main course, the longest of the five stories by far, but it had me in the palm of its hand right away.

The banal garden party for all of the academics, introducing us to Dexter Stanley (Fritz Weaver), Henry Northrup (Hal Holbrook), and, of course, Henry's wife Wilma "Just call me Billie, everyone does" (Adrienne Barbeau) had the right amount of entertaining set-up, but that wasn't the scene that charged me up and burrowed under my skin.

You see, Fritz Weaver's Dexter Stanley leaves the party after getting a phone call from Mike the janitor (Don Keefer) at Amberson Hall. He's found something there and he needs a higher-up from the college to take a look at it with him. There is something about the prolonged suspense sequence that follows, with Dexter and janitor Mike looking through the grate under the hallway staircase and then carrying the mysterious crate into the lab that feels like cinematic alchemy to me. All of the meticulous loosening of screws and nails. A flashlight searching for Mike's lost "fuck-a-diddle" quarter. A centuries-old padlock put aside because it might be valuable. And once again the mix of old and new music gives the whole sequence a heightening feeling of suspense, not to mention that it happens in almost real time (there are very few time cuts), and you're starting to get anxious wondering: what the hell is going to be inside this thing?

And then it chirps, almost like a bird. Mike sees something inside the crate and, thinking it might be jewels, hastily reaches inside…and all hell breaks loose. He screams and the lighting instantly goes full primary colors: the deepest red and the bluest blue lighting I had ever seen in a movie.

Dexter tries to save poor Mike from the Savini nightmare inside the crate, but it's no use. And it isn't enough that Mike is mortally wounded and left for dead, no, "Fluffy", the man-eating Tasmanian Devil monster inside the crate, goes on to swallow him whole, sucking him in until even his kicking feet disappear past the lid; the scene punctuated brilliantly by the shorting out of an electrical socket due to it being unceremoniously drenched with Mike's blood.

I couldn't believe what I was seeing. I didn't know why the entire lighting scheme changed when things went haywire, but I loved it. In fact, after this scene, young-me knew two things: (1) every movie I wanted to make going forward was going to be a horror anthology, and (2) when things got hyper-scary, I was going to do Dutch angles and crazy colored lighting. (And when I tried to make home movie productions with my friends, these two rules would usually remain firm, albeit without much success in terms of ever finishing said home movie projects.)

"The Crate" is my absolute favorite story in my absolute favorite horror movie, hands down. The fate of poor Charlie Gereson; Dexter Stanley's histrionics as he tries to explain what happened; the cross-cutting of Wilma's reading of Henry's note while Henry mops up the blood drenched floors of Amberson Hall (accompanied by John Harrison's inspired piano riff on the soundtrack); Henry's involuntarily burst of laughter in the stairwell when he realizes that Wilma has completely fallen for his lie; "Just tell it to call you Billie"...I know every beat of every second of "The Crate" and have for almost 35 years now. It remains one of my favorite anthology segments of all time.

And then E.G. Marshall shows up and steals the whole movie with his performance. He can't even be upstaged by hundreds of thousands of cockroaches. "They're Creeping Up on You" is the perfect bug-coated cherry on top of *Creepshow*, with Marshall's utterly vulgar Upson Pratt a villain for the ages. And yet you can't help but laugh at his stunning nastiness. The man's unfiltered heartlessness is hysterical (the closest thing we get to a sympathetic comment from Upson Pratt is the moment he tells an underling over the speakerphone to "go out and fuck somebody, but wear a rubber, everyone has the damn herpes these days") and makes his eventual fate, a show-stopping practical effect from maestro Savini and a thousand more cockroaches, a gag-inducing delight. Sometimes the audience really, truly, desperately wants to see a thousand cockroaches explode from the mouth and chest of the despicable villain, even if they didn't realize it.

Creepshow opened the door to my wanting to know more about George Romero. It led me straight to *Night of the Living Dead*, another movie that changed my life, and then to *Dawn of the Dead* and *Knightriders*; movies that latched onto me at a very young age and never let go. It also seemed to set off a resurgence in the '80s of anthology TV shows, starting with *Tales from the Darkside*, itself a Romero-produced, spiritual spin-off of *Creepshow,* and carrying through to shows like *Monsters, Tales from the Crypt, Amazing Stories*, the new *Hitchcock Presents*, the new *Twilight Zone*; shows I would stay up late to watch and then watch over and over again on videotape (and collect on DVD decades later).

I even started writing my own short horror stories and overly ambitious horror anthology screenplays. Romero and King opened the floodgates on my creativity. They taught me that a horror movie could not only be about anything but it could be about multiple things within the confines of the same feature!

And it was all because *Creepshow* infected me and made me fall in love with the horror anthology.

At this point in my life, I have one produced feature that is not an anthology but it's a horror-thriller that bears a passing resemblance to Romero's *Night of the Living Dead*, while I have spent the last few years writing and directing horror podplays (scary radio shows) for a show called Earbud Theater. And every time out of the gate, I hope that the next one might be judged *Creepshow*-worthy by my listenership (a recent episode of mine undeniably owes a debt of gratitude to "The Lonesome Death of Jordy Verrill").

I don't think there is one movie that I have watched more often than *Creepshow*. I have spotted every cameo appearance of the marble ashtray (which really does turn up in all five stories and the wraparound – it shows up in Jordy Verrill twice) and have gone back to forgetting that Bingo O'Malley plays all of the supporting characters in Jordy. It's a movie I can't get enough of. I think that whenever I am watching an anthology movie or TV episode, my not-so-secret hope is that it will give me the same visceral thrill that *Creepshow* did. Maybe this time, I'll have the most fun I've ever had being scared. Or maybe *Creepshow* was really it.

THE EVIL DEAD

BY
TRISTA ROBINSON

Actor/Producer
Purgatory Road, The Human Race,
Silent Retreat, Echoes of Fear
Facebook: @TristaRobinsonPage
Twitter: @TristaRobinson

My favorite horror film is *The Evil Dead*. There, I said it. As us horror geeks know all too well, choosing a favorite can be emotionally draining. I may sound dramatic, but hey, I am an actor. I love horror, but I especially love *The Evil Dead*. This must be what it is like to have a favorite child. Sure, you love them all, and sure, you give them all the same amount of attention, but deep down...

Anyway. This film has meant different things to me over the span of my life. As an actor, arcs are important. I approach each script by trying to decipher my character's arc. Of course I do a lot more, but the arc is a huge and often challenging part of the process. *The Evil Dead* and I, we have a great arc.

When I was a kid, it was just me and my Dad for several years, until he remarried. Besides riding on the back of his motorcycle, my favorite pastime was watching horror together. Oh man, did he love *The Evil Dead* and its successors. This was not just horror, it was fun! The film does not take itself too seriously and is not subtle. Perfect for a small child. Well, for me at least. As an adult, this film has affected my life in an entirely different way. As someone who specializes in indie horror, I know all too well what a difficult marathon making a low budget movie can be. The production of *Evil Dead* was fraught with difficulties and exemplifies overcoming the odds. How is it simultaneously amateur and amazing?! It is so far from perfect and I love it all the more because of it. I cannot say that *The Evil Dead* consciously inspired me to become an actor, because it really only brought me joy and comfort (yes, comfort) as a child. Only later did I really glean inspiration and motivation from my knowledge of the production, while working on low budget indie horror shoots.

While studying at a conservatory in New York, I was embarrassed of my love for all things horror. There was seemingly nobody else there who shared my interests, and that sort of work was not taken seriously. I moved to L.A. and made no effort to pursue horror specifically or even admit my love of it, but that is what I began to be cast in. So I met more and more people like me. There is a huge horror community and so many devoted horror fans, and horror is, once again, a huge and happy part of my life. I have accidentally solidified my identity and *The Evil Dead* is there for me again, just like when I was a kid, but now in a whole new way. Seems so fateful.

I meet a lot of people and don't really get star struck. I met Bruce Campbell once at a party, and happened to have a copy of his book on hand (cool kids bring books to parties, right?), and was too lame to mention it, let alone ask him to sign it. He was sweet and I was awkward. Best night ever.

I should mention that I didn't really understand the concept of tree rape as a kid, I just thought that silly lady was being attacked by a tree. I should also mention that I have not seen the 2013 remake, so I cannot weigh in on it. Perhaps I should have watched it in preparation for this essay, but I didn't want to. It is like having a pet pass away and then not wanting to get another one right away, except *The Evil Dead* is not dead and this sentence is confusing and maybe this analogy makes no sense. I am not a writer, I am an actor. I am just not ready to watch it ok? It didn't help me bond with my Dad and it didn't inspire me to keep working my ass off in my chosen profession. I am sure it is a good horror flick. Maybe one day I will be ready to give it a shot.

    The Evil Dead may seem like a silly horror movie, but somehow it has always been there for me, even when I was embarrassed by it. I never could have imagined this arc.

    P.S. I do love *Ash vs Evil Dead*!

HALLOWEEN

BY
ALEX NAPIWOCKI

Writer/Director/Production Designer/Musician
Drunk Zombies, Blue Balls, Death House, Altitude,
Anders Manor, Audio Vampire, White Coffin
SafetyMeetingProductions.com Facebook: @Napiwocki
Instagram/Twitter: @AlexNapiwocki

How does one pick a favorite horror film when there are so many? I love the exploitation of the '70s, the pure slasher of the '80s, and the gory melt movies of the early '90s. How do I narrow it down to just one? The only fair way seems to be to choose the one that started this horror obsession in the first place. The granddaddy of them all, the slasher that defines the genre - John Carpenter's *Halloween*.

I grew up as a sick kid - allergies, asthma, the works. This left me with a lot of down time while the other kids were getting brainwashed at school. I'd run the gauntlet of late '80s and early '90s daytime TV. It was cheesy and I was already beginning to hate commercials. They bring you out of fantasy and back into reality, totally ruining the experience. This is why, at a young age, my tastes started moving from television to movies.

My sister, being seven years older, definitely had an impact on the movies and music I would find myself chasing. Through her, I found punk rock at nine, and horror films not long after. One particular illness left me home for a long haul. I had my tonsils removed and I was allergic to the anesthetic they used to put me under. During the surgery, my heart literally stopped. I was on bed rest for weeks. Blockbuster couldn't keep up with me and I was running out of new releases left and right.

My sister had a best friend with quite the movie collection. He also had two VCRs hooked up to each other. One day, he sent a stack of VHS tapes through my sister to help me heal. Little did I know that they would change my life forever. One tape had a couple skate punk flicks, *Thrashin'* and *Gleaming The Cube*, both of which I still love to this day. But those are guilty pleasures, not the Holy Grail. *Halloween 1-6* were also in the stack, and holy shit, was life about to be worth living.

I'd seen some horror flicks and had an idea what the *Halloween* movies were. I knew about the Jason movies and the Chucky movies. Most of the horror films I'd seen were part of the ghost, vampire, or werewolf genres. None of those prepared me for what was about to take place. I began watching *Halloween*. Seeing Michael Myers take the screen was the first time I was truly terrified watching a film.

Halloween is not a movie that requires gore. It's the fear of what's behind you that makes this film truly terrifying. Michael doesn't move like a man. He doesn't move like a maniacal monster either. He moves like only Michael Myers can: smooth, stealth and calculated. He doesn't have any cheesy catchphrases. In fact, he never says a word, and it makes him so much creepier than any other horror icon.

There's more to *Halloween* than Michael Myers to make it my favorite. Jamie Lee Curtis is the quintessential final girl. No one can match her innocence and strength. Following Laurie Strode (played by Curtis) through Haddonfield is how us viewers became locals. The town and Michael are both viewed through her eyes. Her cat and mouse game with Myers is amongst the best in horror history. I spent a couple weeks just watching *Halloween* over and over. I had the whole series up to the Paul Rudd as Tommy Doyle one, but the first flick, I watched twice as much as the rest combined. It has the best characters and the best scares. The music is next level, the lighting is eerie, and the locations are haunting. It's everything one should strive for when making a horror film.

When the curator of this collection of essays, Christian Ackerman, gave me this task, I don't think he knew how much he was involved in making *Halloween* my favorite horror film. He accidentally (or knowing him, quite purposely) taught me the fundamentals of film. He did this by giving me a bunch of VHS tapes in the '90s, and it all started with this one perfectly scary flick.

Flash forward to 2015: I filmed my first short film as a writer and director. A trash comedy Halloween slasher titled *The Curse Of The Glamulet*. My inspirations at the time were definitely more John Waters and Troma than classic horror or even slashers, but the model was *Halloween*. My film turned into its own take on the final girl and the *Halloween* slasher. I was even compelled to name the main character Lori. 40 years later, the film industry still pays homage to this flick. I literally wouldn't be making films or writing this essay without it. Sorry Jason. Sorry Freddy. My favorite horror movie is, without a doubt, *Halloween*.

DAWN OF THE DEAD

BY
CHUCK FOSTER

Screenwriter/Journalist/Musician
Film Threat, The Summoners, Hell's Belles,
Pide Ayuda, Lugal
Twitter: @MrPhreek Instagram: @Chuck.Foster.184
Facebook: @PideAyudaBand

The screen looks like raw ground meat. An ominous tone recalling Stan Kenton's *City of Glass* resounds and the camera zooms back to reveal a woman sleeping against a carpeted wall. She's having a nightmare, wakes up shouting and someone grabs her, asks if she's okay. She's at work, a news talk show where the host and crew are mocking the guest who pleads with them to understand him, while the show's producer knowingly broadcasts incorrect information on rescue stations in order to facilitate ratings.

And so begins George A. Romero's *Dawn of the Dead*, my favorite film of all time.

My father first showed me the movie when I was in fourth

grade, about eight or nine years old. You may think that's too young, but my father was a horror host on TV (Grimsley if you must know), and horror is his mode of expression. He showed me *The Shining* when I was four years old, which gave me nightmares for three months, pissed off my mother, but forever altered my psyche, so *Dawn of the Dead* was tame by comparison.

It consumed my nine-year-old mind, to the extent that I recited the entire story to my friends and killing zombies became our primary mode of recess play. It had everything – action, zombies and amazing music, and I was hooked. I wanted to be Peter, a 6'5" black man, played by Ken Foree, the best hero I'd ever seen anywhere and it didn't matter that I was a white suburban kid. I also wanted to live in a mall, not because I liked mall culture, but because they truly were modern castles where you could survive if left to your own devices.

To call it prophetic is an understatement. The opening TV station broadcast is exactly what would happen on CNN today. The National Guard raiding projects for housing the undead? Give it time. The police abandoning their post during Armageddon? Probable. Rednecks using their Second Amendment right to use walkers as target practice? Duh. Motorcycle gangs raiding a clearly established outpost? Well, Rick Grimes blindly raided and mass murdered a savior's outpost in *The Walking Dead* and he's considered the good guy.

But there's so much more. Just look at the characters.

Fran, played by the beautiful Gaylen Ross, opens the film. Essentially, it's her story. She's the archetypal '70s woman: raised to believe in a paternal society, but quickly inspired to break that mold. She stands up to her boss in the TV station for his fraudulent broadcasts. When it comes to violence, she's not sure what to do, as when her boyfriend unexpectedly meets some zombies in the country. She soon learns from the mistake however, and expresses her interest learning how to use firearms properly, to the extent that the men trust her to handle major anti-undead missions and she gets Steven to teach her how to fly the helicopter. She's also pregnant.

Steven, her boyfriend, played by the highly underrated David Emge, thinks highly of himself. He's a hotshot traffic reporter who happens to fly a helicopter, their primary mode of transportation. He wants to be one of the guys, but he's a horrible shot and kind of a douchebag. Status means something to him – after they've conquered the mall, he picks up a coat and rolls his eyes at the price – and eventually this drives him apart from Fran, to the point where she won't even accept his post-apocalyptic marriage proposal. Maybe they were never meant to be together to begin with, but now they're stuck together for better or for worse, whether they like it or not. He also brings about their downfall as masters of the mall by shooting at the raiders because, according to him, "It's ours." His greed leads to his being overcome by zombies but, even though he knows he won't live, he's still vain enough to not kill himself to make sure he doesn't come back. He actually leads the zombies back to their hidden lair, either from instinct or spite.

Roger (Scott H. Reiniger), is Steven's friend and the only other person he's asked to join him in his helicopter escape from reality. He's in the National Guard and violence excites him, perhaps a bit too much, leading to his demise as his frivolous behavior leads to his death. Watching his fellow officers abuse their power in the projects makes him sick, but he quickly gets too cocky in claiming the mall and gets bitten by a zombie. He knows he's going to die and, while in a state of delirium, begs the one person he trusts with a gun, Peter, to take care of him when he comes back as a zombie. In fact, throughout his entire sickness, he wants Peter with him, showing how much he thinks of Steven, aka Flyboy.

Finally, there's Peter, my cool, calm and collected hero. He's from the projects and gets so disgusted by the abuse of his fellow officers during the raid that he finally kills one who is going haywire. Afterward, he quickly escapes to the basement to be alone, but Roger ends up there after also running to the basement in disgust. Here, they bond while meeting a one-legged priest who tells them, "We must stop the killing or we lose the war." Later, Peter reveals his Trini heritage and talks about his grandfather, a voodoo priest who warned that the dead would walk the earth "when there's no more room in hell." He also doesn't care much for Steven, who almost accidentally shot him while they were on the run, even revealing a slight smile when he kills the zombie version, but he also considers killing himself afterward. Thankfully, he changes his mind and fights through rooms of zombies to join Fran in the helicopter and they ride off into the sunrise.

Then there are the subjects of racism, consumerism and violence, which are handled in an entirely subversive, nonchalant way and still resound in the modern atmosphere.

First, there's Wooly, the big, angry, racist National Guardsman who runs rampant in the projects, kicking in doors and killing whatever he sees, alive or dead. He represents the core of America - the Fox News and Trump supporters who have always been around, but always felt marginalized by the liberal cities. He says and does everything they wish they could do in real life. Ultimately, he gets taken out by one of his own men, Peter, who nobody stops.

Then there's the dock police led by an unnamed sergeant, played by the underrated Joseph Pilato (Rhodes from *Day of the Dead*). Steven lands on their dock to refuel, finds the post to be empty and investigates, discovering the radio operator has either been attacked by zombies or his face was blown out by a bullet. Eventually, they make themselves known to Flyboy and Fran in a threatening manner. They recognize him, but want to know what they're doing there and who's in the car approaching the dock while they're trying to escape. Eventually, they make peace and agree to go their separate ways, the police just trying to make it to "the island" ("What island?" "Any island.").

Next, there's the rednecks throughout Central Pennsylvania, who see the whole thing as target practice. George Romero has publicly stated that these people scared him more than the zombies. They drink coffee and beer and barbeque and go out for a hunt. Not much more is seen beyond that, but a lot is implied. Ironically, they seem to have the most stable setting at the time of their appearance in the film.

A talk show appears for a while on the Emergency Broadcast Channel. Howard Smith plays the disheveled TV announcer while Richard France (previously of a brilliant role in Romero's *The Crazies*) portrays an eccentric, possibly insane, eye-patched scientist. Their exchanges relay the deteriorated state of civilization, culminating in France's scientist proclaiming they should either feed the undead or drop nuclear bombs. Soon after, the channel is no longer broadcasting.

Finally, there's the motorcycle raiders (foreshadowed by Peter when he says "That whirlybird on the roof might give us away"), who discover the mall by watching Fran learn how to fly the helicopter. They try to talk their way in, claiming there's just three of them, but Peter and Steven go to the roof and see the legion of motorcycle lights heading toward them. Initially, the plan is to let them come in with the zombies, take what they want and leave, but it turns violent when Steven gets jealous and fires on them. They're actually a continuation of the aforementioned rednecks, six months down the line, evolved into a motorcycle-driven army. Tom Savini, who produced the effects for the film, plays one of the gang's leaders. He shoves his trademark machete into the grill and yells, "I see you, Chocolate Man!" when he chases Peter into the hidden ducts used to get in and out of the mall area. Peter eventually assassinates him, then escapes to the helicopter with Fran while the zombies feast on the corpses of numerous motorcycle raiders.

The zombies themselves, of course, represent consumer culture as they literally consume everything in their path. Steven ironically acknowledges that the undead are drawn to the mall because it "was an important place in their lives." Ultimately however, humanity is the greatest enemy – we defeat ourselves in times of crisis.

Visually, *Dawn of the Dead* reaches the pinnacle of what George Romero called his "cover your ass" style of filmmaking, a method he lost over the past forty years. He used this ideology to great effect in all his films from *Night of the Living Dead* to *Knightriders*, creating a signature visual style that was both gritty and fluid with a constantly flowing stream of edits. It even transfers to the comic book quality Romero always said marked the movie. Unfortunately, he lost it with *Day of the Dead* - a great film, but the first to stray from the Romero mold.

Favorite version? Definitely the "extended" cut, the original 139 minutes he sent to Cannes. Then Argento's fast-paced European version, which featured many of the alternate takes used in the internet "Ultimate Fan" cut. Ironically, I think Romero's preferred version, the 127-minute theatrical cut is the lesser of the four as it leaves out a lot of the elements that made the extended so powerful. The scene where Roger and Peter fully bond while killing the zombies protected by the tenants is longer and more emotional, and the police dock gets butchered to where it doesn't really make any sense. There's also a lot of footage missing that shows the extent of their boredom living in the mall and clips of barbarity depicting the true brutality of the motorcycle gang. Once I saw those additional twelve minutes, I could never go back to the theatrical cut.

As for the remake, I actually liked it. It was certainly one of the better remakes produced for the ADD generation, with an excellent cast and some truly disgusting gore. Unfortunately, it completely lacked any of the social commentary of the original, making it a vapid fast zombie action movie rather than powerful examination of American culture.

Sadly, George A. Romero died on July 16, 2017. His final film was 2009's *Survival of the Dead*, a movie so bad it made direct-to-DVD zombie flicks look good. I always hoped he'd ditch the zombie trap, something he'd created and owned, but only returned to for money, in favor of something more personal shot in the "cover your ass" style of filmmaking that made him so innovative in his early films. It never happened.

I would have been the first in line.

A NIGHTMARE ON ELM STREET 3: DREAM WARRIORS

BY
CHRISTIAN ACKERMAN

Producer/Writer/Director
Hell's Belles, Bethany, Death House, Deadly Reunion
Slayer: Pride in Prejudice & You Against You
Twitter/Instagram: @Ackronomicon

The year: 1988. One of my two best friends in elementary school, Eddie Hernandez, was riding his yellow and blue dirt bike to my place for a sleepover. Little did I know, it would be the night that changed the course of my life forever.

Earlier that day, I asked Eddie, "Do you have any movies to bring?" He replied, "I have a copy of *A Nightmare on Elm Street 3: Dream Warriors.*" Oh, hell no. That was NOT what I wanted to hear. You see, a few years earlier, when I was about eight, I snuck a peek as my mom watched the original *A Nightmare on Elm Street.* I got about two minutes into the opening boiler room dream sequence before I got the fuck out of that living room and SWORE I'd never watch a Freddy Krueger movie. But by the time Eddie rolled through that night, I was older. I was 11. Maybe it was about time I overcame that fear. It was time to face Freddy full-on.

When Eddie arrived, he pulled out a VHS in a black clamshell with a white slip of paper that read "Movies To Go." That store was my childhood movie university. I spent hours there, sifting through the titles, discovering cool new movies, while finding the ones that my parents wanted to teach me about. Movies To Go also allowed us to write our phone numbers on the backs of their magnificent new release standees and posters. When the films were no longer new releases, they would call and let me know my claimed items were ready for pick up! Just imagine owning a giant cardboard standee for *Freddy's Dead: The Final Nightmare*, *Cape Fear*, or *Darkman*. I had all three in my bedroom!

Knowing that Eddie didn't go to the store that day, I asked him, "How did you get *Dream Warriors*?" Eddie replied, "Jared stole it." Now, this made it even more taboo for me. We were to watch a Freddy movie that the cool kid across the street stole! Jared was the best friend of Eddie's brother Danny. (Being three years older, they were usually too-cool to hang with us.) About Eddie: he wasn't the type to peer pressure you. But, I also wasn't about to be a wuss and not watch a movie stolen by the cool kids! I was going to watch this movie, with one caveat: Eddie had to warn me about scary parts so I could cover my eyes. I figured, at the very least, I can finally say I saw a Freddy movie.

We fed the black tape into the machine and pressed play...

Now, let me provide a bit of insight to my identity as a child. I grew up in Santa Maria (a fairly small town in California) as a slightly above-average athelete and an excellent student. On the playground, I wasn't a fighter, but I'd play up the role of a psychopath to my friends for comedic purposes. My dad raised my brother and I in the world of camping, fishing, and hunting. He taught us the proper handling of weapons to keep yourself and everyone around you safe. I was shooting guns by the age of four, and earned my adult hunting license at the age of nine. I learned how to clean and gut the birds, fish, and mammals I killed. I witnessed the stringing up and gutting of deer and wild boars. I watched bulls getting castrated and cows giving birth on our friend's dairy farm. None of this phased me. It was part of my being. I had these horrors of flesh and death around me as a kid, but I was afraid of horror films. As an adult, I've only now grown to make these connections of life and death to my enjoyment of fictional horror.

My dad never liked watching horror movies. He saw things he didn't want to face when watching them. He'd tell us that he saw enough horror in his life. He was in car accidents where his friends flew out of the car and their brains were scattered on the asphalt before him. He likely had many more incidents that he never even told us about. On the other hand, my mom loved watching horror films. She always found them thrilling, although she'd have to watch them when my dad wasn't around! I remember renting and watching *Faces of Death* with her and my friends. Now, that's how to parent!

As I sat with Eddie that night, totally unprepared for the nightmare-fueling madness in store for me, he would forewarn me when Freddy was set to kill. During the first death or two, I listened in palm-induced blackness. After a while, I realized something. Freddy wasn't solely a horrible demonic dude. He was quite the character! He was quite the villain! Above all, he was quite the comedian! I found out that he had a huge sense of humor! I loved *Ghostbusters, Gremlins, Blazing Saddles,* and *Airplane*; but, for the first time, I realized that these movies were all connected with a sense of humor! Essentially, horror is about death, but it can also be a funny roller-coaster. It could be me playing make-believe psycho on the playground for laughs. Horror could be anything I wanted it to be!

As *Dream Warriors* played, I instantly connected with the characters. These were the rebellious outsiders; the "crazies" who couldn't deal with life in "normal" society. They had issues. Issues that weren't properly acknowledged by the adults. They were the perfect cool kids. Teens that put on their bad-motherfucker fronts, yet had tender sides and issues that the adults couldn't quite understand. As the film progresses, you realize they're all being tormented by the same entity: a demonic former human out to exploit their dreams of success and destroy them. This maniac was the product of their parents' secret past; an evil the kids couldn't understand without talking to their elders and dealing with those demons (hopefully before Freddy got to them!).

After finishing *Dream Warriors*, I had a completely new sense of being. I had conquered what I had called my greatest fear up to that point: I saw a Freddy movie! I watched the first two films. I became obsessed with Freddy, convincing my mom to spend the money to buy me a mask, glove and sweater, under the guise that she wouldn't have to buy me a Halloween costume for the next three years. (I lived up to that promise!) I began turning in short stories for writing assignments (with storylines plucked straight from the films) about Freddy killing people! I would draw murder scenes from the films and turn them in with the stories. Somehow, the teachers never sent me to the school psychologist for any of this! They gave me As!

Over the years, I've often wondered what actually made my mind demented enough to like horror. Was it my sometimes macabre, attention-getting social skills? Was it the fact that I once had no qualms about killing, gutting, and eating other creatures? Was it all a front to gain attention? Or, was I just a smart-ass weirdo who had finally found a passion: relishing in the demise of mankind? It really could be all of these, but while writing this essay, I made another connection concerning my mental and artistic evolution to an event involving someone else altogether: Jared.

Not long after Eddie showed me *Dream Warriors*, he was over for another sleepover. This time, we were watching an HBO comedy special by some random comedian. My dad, out working in the garage, came in and asked "Did you hear that?" I asked "Hear what?" He said, "It sounded like a gunshot." Obviously, my dad knew what a gunshot sounded like. He shrugged it off and we went back to our show...until we heard the sirens.

The ambulance and cop cars stopped right in front of Jared's house. Knowing his brother Danny was having a sleepover there that night, Eddie went over to investigate. As I stayed back to observe from my side of the street, I saw Danny drift out onto the porch and hang his head in his hands. Eddie consoled him. I knew this was bad. After a while, the coroners wheeled Jared out of the house with nothing but a bloodied white sheet over his body. He was dead. Apparently, while his parents were away, he decided to show-off in front of Danny by playing Russian Roulette with his dad's gun, loaded with one blank round. If he had proper gun training, he'd know never to fucking play with guns (along with the fact that blanks fire enough explosive discharge to kill you at close range).

Eddie went home with his brother that night, and I was left alone in my room to sleep. I always had trouble sleeping at night, usually from fear of monsters or psycho killers entering with criminal intent. This time, after crawling into bed, the events of the night finally hit me. I burst into tears. My mom came in to console me. Up until this point, my life was tragedy-free. Now, this wasn't make-believe. I had finally experienced the humanistic horrors of death...and it was scary.

I'm just now realizing that seeing Jared get wheeled out of his house on a gurney was a similar scenario that Nancy went through in the first *Elm Street*, when she watched the paramedics and police deal with her boyfriend's death from

222   **CHRISTIAN ACKERMAN**

across the street. Maybe this is what fueled my interest in Freddy. Maybe those films provided a way to escape that real-life horror. To confront it and beat it like I was always afraid to before.

As I grew up, the horror movies that inspired me led me into a desire to make films. At 18, I left home for college in Los Angeles and got straight into the entertainment business. Over the years, I've been fortunate enough to cross paths with some of the great talents that made *Dream Warriors* my favorite horror film. I was cast in a filmmaker competition reality show pilot hosted by none other than Wes Craven. (Spending three days making a horror short as he bestowed his guidance upon my colleagues and I was nothing short of euphoric.) I've gotten to hang with Patricia Arquette and learn an on-set secret of hers that I've never told anyone. I've gotten tipsy and danced with Penelope Sudrow; chilled at a horror convention with my ultimate final girl, Heather Langenkamp; shot the shit with Chuck Russell after engineering a *Movie Crypt* podcast for Joe Lynch and Adam Green; met Frank Darabont at a New Beverly Cinema *Dream Warriors* screening; and the recent big one: stumbled upon Robert Shaye (the man behind all of the *Elm Street* films) at a Screamfest tribute screening of *The Dream Master*, where I proceeded to tell him how much *Nightmare 3* led me to my career. (He was ecstatic to learn that his films inspired me to live creatively for the past 20+ years.)

Each time I meet anyone associated with *Dream Warriors*, I have them sign my most cherished item, an Italian *Nightmare 3* poster, first signed by Patricia with the caption, "Dream on, Dream Warrior." (There's nothing cooler than the final girl from your favorite horror film including you in her Freddy-fighting army!) I always make it a point to thank everyone for their contribution to the film. Their art is why I'm here today. No other moment in my life has been more important to my development than the night Eddie brought over that movie. It sparked something in me that I'm still trying to figure out to this day.

Hanging out with Wes, his gentle nature and intelligence clashed beautifully with his extreme, horrific art. His work showed me that it was okay to explore the darkness within me, and to embrace that monster in a positive and cathartic way through storytelling.

As I get older, I still ask myself, "Why am I into such creepy, fucked-up shit?" Maybe someday, Freddy will explain it to me in my dreams, followed by a sadistic one-liner, four razor-sharp knives to my stomach, and an evil laugh! I can't wait!

Dream on, Dream Warriors!

MY FAVORITE HORROR MOVIE
SCREAM TEAM:

Christian Ackerman has produced over 20 feature films including *Slayer: The Repentless Killogy, Portal, Deadly Reunion, Bethany, Family Vanished,* and two *Stalked By My Doctor* films. As a director, his shorts *Hell's Belles, The Summoners,* and *Watch Your Back* have won over 35 film festival awards.

Designer Josh McKevitt has featured work on several film and TV shows such as *American Horror Story: Cult, Perry Mason, Bliss, Vida* and *The Mindy Project.* One of his many hobbies includes practising prosthetic makeup FX on himself, which led to creating the *My Favorite Horror Movie* cover mascot, Uncle Crusty. He currently resides in Los Angeles with his fiancé Gabrielle and their Welsh "Terror" dog, Lemon.

Made in United States
North Haven, CT
16 October 2021